DAILY HEALING BREAD
From God's Table

NANCY DUFRESNE

Ed Dufresne Ministries
Murrieta, California

Daily Healing Bread From God's Table
ISBN 0-940763-11-7
Copyright 1997 by
Ed Dufresne Ministries
P.O. Box 1010
Murrieta, CA 92564

Visit our website at: www.eddufresne.org

Published by
El Dufresne Ministries
P.O. Box 1010
Murrieta, CA 92564

Editorial Consultant: Phyllis Mackall, Broken Arrow, OK.

DEDICATION

❧

This book is lovingly dedicated to my husband, Ed,
who has faithfully carried God's healing power
to thousands of sick and afflicted souls.
He has not only been an example of Christ
for me to follow,
but he is my mentor in the faith.

CONTENTS

❧

AUTHOR'S PREFACE

❦

And He (Jesus) *said to them, Be careful what you
are hearing. The measure [of thought and study]
you give [to the truth you hear] will be the measure
[of virtue* (power) *and knowledge] that comes back
to you, and more [besides] will be given to you who
hear.*

Mark 4:24 (The Amplified Bible)

In this scripture, Jesus reveals how to increase the
measure of healing power that flows into your body. The
more you give yourself to hearing, meditating upon,
thinking about, studying, and acting upon divine healing
truths, the greater the measure of healing power that will
flow into your body.

A. B. Simpson makes a statement in his book, The
Gospel of Healing, that is so foundational to faith, all
believers would do well to take it to heart: "The new life
must be kept by constant abiding in Him, and receiving
from Him. It is not a permanent deposit, but a **constant
dependence.**"

Paul's writings reflect that same understanding in
Acts 17:28: *"For in him we live, and move, and have our
being."*

God's plan is for every move in a believer's life to be
authored and directed by Him. We are to look to God
moment by moment for the constant inflow of His sus-
taining life. That life will then guide and direct every
move we make. The final result will be that our entire
being will be affected and filled with the fullness of God.

This is the three-step process Paul stated in Acts 17:28.
If we continually draw our life from Him, it will affect our
every move, and then our entire being will be filled with
Him.

The believer who walks in ongoing health draws his or
her health from the Word of God on a daily basis.
Proverbs 4:22 tells us, *"For they* (His words) *are life unto those*

that find them and health (medicine) *to all their flesh."*

If natural medicine is taken on a daily basis, it will perform its purpose, but if it is taken sporadically, it loses its effectiveness. This is also true of the Word of God.

If a daily dosage of God's healing Word is consumed by a sick person, it will also perform its purpose, which is health to that body. But if it is taken sporadically, its power and effectiveness is diluted by a lukewarm attitude.

In Mark 7:24-30, when the Syrophoenician woman requested healing from Jesus for her demon-possessed daughter, Jesus responded by saying, *"Let the children first be filled: for it is not meet to take the children's bread, and to cast it unto the dogs"* (verse 27).

We can see in this passage that Jesus called healing "the children's bread."

In prayer, Jesus requested the Father, *"Give us this day our daily bread."* Jesus taught that it is a daily diet of healing bread that brings and maintains health in believers' bodies.

With this in mind, this book is brought to you. It contains servings of healing bread spread on the table where the saints of God are fed. It contains daily portions for you to feast on and savor in your thought life throughout the day.

These portions will bring health to a sick body, peace to a tormented mind, and joy to a depressed soul.

Meditate upon these portions all day long. Ponder these truths of God's Word deeply. Repeat them to yourself throughout the day, and let His medicine do its work in your body. Let each truth soak deeply into your spirit.

The revelations of God's Word are so life-changing, we do ourselves a great injustice to read a book simply to get through it. We should study the Word to gain revelation, for it is only lived revelation that will ever change us.

As the old song says:

> *"Come and dine," the Master calleth, "Come and dine."*
> *You can feast at Jesus' table all the time.*
> *He who fed the multitude, turned the water into wine,*
> *To the hungry calleth now, "Come and dine."*

INTRODUCTION

❧

The Spirit of God has been faithful to be my Teacher, Counselor, and Guide, especially during times of tests and trials, revealing the truths and depths of God's Word to my understanding and stating them in words of such simplicity, they found their home in my heart and their results in my life.

These truths were so precious to me, I wrote them down for fear of losing even one of the revelations He brought. This book is a collection of those notes.

The boldface scripture or statement that begins each day's entry was given to me by the Spirit of God. The explanation and teaching is found in the text that follows.

I believe the truths expressed in this book will strengthen your faith, and you will see the necessity of beginning and ending your day with the healing nuggets found within these pages.

After reading this book, begin it again. Keep the river of the healing Word continually flowing through your life and body, because that is the price of constant victory.

May the words and thoughts contained in this book be as liberating to you as they are to me!

Nancy Dufresne
Temecula, California

Daily Healing Bread From God's Table

❧

GOD'S ABIDING PRESENCE

*Divine health and divine healing are nothing
more than the outflow of the divine life within
permeating your body.*

Much needs to be said to the Body of Christ concerning abiding in the presence of God.

It needs to be understood that God's divine presence and power is everywhere, but the believer must also be ever mindful of His presence within and His presence around.

Living in constant fellowship and communion with the Father is the lifetime vocation of the believer, causing his or her every thought and action to focus on the presence of the Father.

If the believer were really mindful of God living inside him, would he ever be able to walk into a movie theater that flashes seductive behavior and profane speech into his eyes and ears, polluting the temple of God?

How it must grieve the heart of God that His children take little or no recognition of His indwelling presence!

Does a believer dare to seek healing from His hand, yet choose to remain so mindless of His life within?

Would that conversation be spoken over the telephone if the Christian really understood that Christ is hearing every word?

Is the indwelling of this precious One so unnoticed that brother would speak against brother without fear and trembling?

If we allow ourselves to be so unmoved by His holy presence within us, how can we ever be expected to move a lost world toward God?

Do believers not yet understand that the flow of this divine life within is dependent upon a constant, continual fellowship and abiding with Christ? Moment by moment, hour by hour, day by day is still not enough time to fathom the depths of His unsearchable riches.

The greatest mystery Paul revealed to the Church by the Holy Spirit is the revelation that God dwells in us!

Without this revelation, no healing can be obtained, no bondage broken, and no enemy stopped. This is the truth on which the entire fellowship of God and man hinges.

Attacks and onslaughts of the enemy go virtually unnoticed when this revelation takes hold of your life!

Anyone who endeavors to seek divine healing apart from seeking the Healer Divine will be sadly disappointed. It is not the doctrine of divine healing alone that brings you deliverance; it is knowing this glorious Healer. He alone is the Healing Balm of Gilead spoken of in scripture.

True joy lies in waking in the morning with Him as the brightness of your day, taking each step throughout the day in reverent fear and trembling of thinking upon anything that would displease Him, and while laying your head on your pillow at night, being so hungry to know Him that the pillow becomes to you the bosom of Jesus that John the apostle reclined upon.

How heartbreaking it must be to Jesus to have His own children give more effort and thought to obtaining His blessings than to obtaining the Pearl of Great Price first.

SEEK YE FIRST THE KINGDOM OF GOD,
and his righteousness and all these things shall
be added unto you.

Matthew 6:33

Jesus tells us that the kingdom of God is within us. Therefore, we must seek to know the One who lives within. We must purpose to follow Him every step throughout the day, and then the healing we desire will be added unto us.

May our desire be like Paul's, when he said, *"That I may know him...."* Herein lies the secret to living in divine health!

❦

THE PRESENCE OF GOD

"Mine enemies...shall fall and perish at thy presence."
Psalm 9:3

Heaven is my destination, but His presence is my
Companion for the journey.

The place of absolute, ongoing victory is found in only one place: the presence of God!

The presence of God is not a feeling; it's a place! Yet when I am in that place, there is the feeling of His presence. We are never to seek the feeling. We are always to seek to be found "in the place."

Where is that place?

It's the place to which I mount when my thoughts and mouth are full of His Word. It's the realm where I soar when He is all I allow my eyes to look upon. It's the mountaintop I abide on when I am more conscious of Him than I am of those around me.

How does one live in that place?

Complete surrender is the road that takes us there.

It's a road with no shortcuts — a road surrounded by distractions that would try to divert us — but, most of all, it's a narrow road. Although we are not allowed to carry anything of self with us on this journey, we are not left alone. We have a Guide — the precious Holy Spirit — who leads the way.

Heaven is my destination, but His presence is my

Companion for the journey. He reveals and shows me things in my life that must be discarded and stripped away if the journey is to continue. He helps me clear from my view things that would cloud the vision of my destination.

He walks with me, leading and guiding me to heaven, to forever remain in the presence of God. He gives us His presence to journey with us on the road that brings us to His presence.

For God's guidance to be effective, this Companion must be talked to, worshipped, adored, and trusted. The more this is done, the more real His presence becomes to us.

When intrusions from the enemy try to block my way, I remain hidden in His presence, and my enemies fall at His feet.

Is it any wonder at all that:

There shall no evil befall thee, neither shall any plague come nigh thy dwelling.

Psalm 91:10

As long as I stay hidden in His presence, I cannot be found by the enemy, for no evil can pass beyond His presence to reach me.

Fear no evil — only fear not being found in His presence!

...[His presence] shall be my dwelling place.

Psalm 23:6 (The Amplified Bible)

❦

LOOKING
UNTO JESUS

*Your healing will manifest when you see Jesus
instead of your symptoms!*

"Looking unto Jesus" is the only rightful place we
are to look, according to God's holy Word
(Hebrews 12:2).

Being more conscious of Him than our symptoms is
how we "rise up on the wings of eagles."

This is only accomplished through great effort on
our part, because every hindrance and stumbling block
the enemy lays in our path is designed to keep our
attention focused on the wrong things.

Through giving ourselves to much Bible study and
fellowship with God, we are able to cause our gaze to
remain fixed on Him when the voice of pain and symptoms screams, trying to divert our attention.

In studying the three Hebrew men who were thrown
into the fiery furnace, I cannot help but realize that for
them to be unaffected by the fire, their gaze had to be
fixed upon God instead of on the fire! What you see is
what will dominate you!

King Nebuchadnezzar, who had cast them into that
fiery furnace, saw the Fourth Man in the midst of the
fire, and saw them make their exit from the fire. When
all you see while in the fire is Jesus, that's when you will
be coming out of that trial!

Even the fire burns cool on the one who doesn't
notice it.

❦

MEDITATE

"This book of the law shall not depart out of thy mouth;
but thou shalt meditate therein day and night..."
Joshua 1:8

Too often we fail to realize the effort that must be put forth to obtain what is rightfully ours as believers. Thank God we have been taught we can have what we say, although some take that as a license to be slothful in their responsibility to the Word.

True faith is not just a confession; it is a lifestyle!

One day as I was thinking about Mark 11:23, the Spirit of God brought my attention to the last line of that verse: *"...he shall have whatsoever he saith."*

The Spirit of God said to me, "The more you say it, the more you will have it!" That shows me we are the ones who determine the measure we receive.

People who are highly educated in their fields take years to study and prepare for service. Can we rightly give less to our divine lifestyle and vocation?

Jesus said, "Follow me, and I will make you fishers of men." Those disciples didn't clock in at 8 o'clock, only to punch out at 5 o'clock sharp! Their training consisted of a lifestyle of eating, traveling, listening, sleeping, and living daily with the Savior while He was on the Earth, and they continued that same lifestyle after Jesus went back to heaven. They knew it took that kind of commitment to be His follower.

Do we dare to presume we could give anything less to the Master and expect to have His full blessing flowing in our lives?

When God tells us to meditate in the Word day and night, He is telling us the length of time we must spend to live as He would have us live – day and night!

To live healed, we must eat, live, and breathe the Word.

The enemy lies to us and tells us the price is too high, or we can't meditate in the Word day and night. God will not tell us to do something we are incapable of doing.

Keep God and His Word foremost in your heart and thoughts, and do nothing to displease Him. This is the lifestyle that brings victory at every turn.

Day and night are not too much for us to give to God, seeing that He has given us eternity with Him!

❧

DETERMINE YOUR POSITION

"I will praise the Lord according to his righteousness..."
Psalm 7:17

Aimee Semple McPherson, who was a noted evangelist from the 1920s until the early 1940s, once held a tent meeting in an area of the United States that was greatly resistant to her meetings and the Pentecostal message.

One evening, dozens of men holding burning torches surrounded her tent, threatening to burn down the tent along with her and the hundreds of people who were in attendance.

The congregation was frightened and sat paralyzed in their seats. The threats were being yelled so loudly that Sister Aimee could not be heard above them, for there were no sound systems in that day.

She silently began to question the Lord about what to do next. The Holy Spirit spoke to her and said, "Just worship the Lord."

She replied, "That's a little hard to do in the middle of these loud threats and the position *I* am in."

God replied, "Don't worship Me because of the position *you're* in, but because of the position *I'm* in!"

As Sister Aimee began to worship, the Lord opened her eyes, and she saw a vision of bats that encircled that tent with wings interlocked.

But as she continued to worship, she saw those bats

recede into the darkness and angels move forward and encircle the tent with their wings interlocked.

The men with the torches ran off, and the power of God fell under the tent.

What is your position today? Are you in pain and suffering with a disease? Worshipping God will drive back the powers of darkness.

Thank God for your health. Thank Him for those stripes that were laid on Jesus to purchase your healing and health.

Let His position determine your position!

HIDDEN IN CHRIST

Giants shrink in size when placed next to God.

Moses sent twelve spies into the land of Canaan, and the Bible states that ten of the twelve brought back an evil report about the land. They said, "The land eateth up the inhabitants." They declared there were giants in the land, and compared to those giants, they were like grasshoppers in their own sight. The Bible called this an "evil report."

What does it matter what you look like in your own sight? Walking in your own power and strength, you will never be able to defeat any strategy of the devil. Your defense lies only in being *"hid with Christ in God"* (Colossians 3:3).

God is in you to put you over; otherwise, you would go under. You are no match for the devil, but the devil is no match for God! Your victory lies in how close you live to God.

Do you rely on His strength to fight your battles? Do you use the weapons He gives?

The ten spies gave an evil report, because they compared the giants to themselves, and they saw defeat. But Joshua and Caleb had a victory report, because they compared those same giants to God and saw no defeat!

There is no victory for the believer who takes his or her eyes off the Victor! Fix your gaze on Jesus, and chart your course for victory.

When you compare yourself to that sickness, you can't win. But when you compare that sickness to Jesus, you have already won, because He has *"...spoiled principalities and powers, he made a show of them openly."*

❦

THE HEALER WITHIN

The Healer is within you, so healing is within you.

A. B. Simpson wrote a fabulous book called *The Gospel of Healing,* in which he gives his testimony of healing.

For years he had suffered from a heart problem. Eventually the best doctors gave up on him, telling him he had six months to live.

At the time, he was the pastor of a large church; however, he had not received the revelation of divine healing. Then he took note that several people in his congregation had been healed by the power of God through other ministries.

Having received such a bleak report from his doctors, Dr. Simpson separated himself from his work and went off to study what the Bible says on the subject of divine healing. Reading from Genesis to Revelation, he found that healing belongs to the believer.

He then prayed the prayer of faith and declared that, according to the Word of God, he was healed. Although the manifestation had not yet come to his body, he believed that healing was his and that it would be manifested in his body in time.

Only days after having prayed this prayer and receiving his healing by faith, he was invited to give a testimony to some men who were on a Christian retreat. As he prepared to deliver the Word, the Spirit of God brought the scripture to him found in Matthew 8:17, *"Himself took our infirmities, and bare our sicknesses."*

Taking this text, he ministered on the word "Himself," explaining that Jesus was the One who had completed the healing work.

He told the gathering how he had come to receive Jesus as his Healer, and that although the doctors had only given him six months to live, he now had a new report to believe, and that according to the Word of God, he believed he had received his healing, regardless of what his physical symptoms told him.

After the meeting, several men invited Dr. Simpson to go with them to climb a nearby mountain. He immediately recalled how his doctors had warned him never to attempt to climb steps, as that act alone would prove to be fatal for him.

He began to decline their offer, but the thought came to him, "You took Jesus as your Healer, and you confessed that you were healed. Can a healed man not climb a mountain?" Dr. Simpson sensed that God was in this, and he agreed to accompany them.

As he began the climb, he felt all the old, familiar pain in his chest and heart. He began to grow dizzy, and he was on the verge of passing out. Then his spirit rose up and he reminded himself, "No, I am healed." He meditated on how Jesus took his infirmities.

As he climbed still farther, the symptoms returned again and again. When Dr. Simpson would turn his attention away from his symptoms and focus back on the Word, the dizziness and pain would leave him.

He continued to climb the mountain, and the battle raged on. He stated that it seemed to him like a roaring lion was walking on one side of him and a peaceful Lamb was walking on the other. The one that he touched was the one that possessed him.

When he reached the top of the mountain, every

pain was gone, never to return. Manifested healing was the reward of his faith.

Thank God, he didn't quit the first time those symptoms flared up. As he said later, "More people lose their healing during the counterattacks than at any other time. Hold fast to your confession of the Word."

Can you hear the roaring of the lion in your ears today? Do symptoms howl and pains persist? Don't be dismayed — the peaceful Lamb is also present! He will never leave you nor forsake you.

Don't listen to the roaring lion, lest you become terrified and faint in your mind.

How much better to be occupied with God and His Word than with a sick body.

Listen to the still, small voice within. He doesn't need to roar to be heard, for He is within you. The Healer is in you, so healing is in you. Give Him your attention and His power will manifest healing in your body.

HIDE AND SEEK

"...your life is hid with Christ..."
Colossians 3:3

*Your words are to be, "No, Satan! I'm hid in
healing, and I'm not coming out!"*

While driving down the road one day, I clearly
heard the Spirit of God speak in my spirit, "Your life is
HID with Christ." He later reminded me of the scripture in I Peter 5:8, *"...your adversary the devil, as a roaring
lion, walketh about, SEEKING whom he may devour."*

Then the Spirit spoke again and said, "There is a
spiritual game of hide-and-seek going on in the lives of
God's people. Satan is seeking you, but God has hid
you in Christ. Stay in Christ, and you can never be
touched."

How that blessed me! I then recalled how I had
often watched my son, Stephen, play hide-and-seek
with his friends. His favorite hiding spot was a closet
beneath the stairway. For some reason, his friends
never noticed that door.

They would run around the house looking for
Stephen and calling his name. As long as he stayed
hidden, he would win. But sometimes the temptation
to see his friends looking for him was too great, and he
would stick his head out from behind that door. When
he did, he would lose, because he came out from his

hiding place.

As long as he stayed in that closet, the door was a cloak that covered him. No matter how much activity was going on around that door, Stephen was still hidden.

Satan wants to lure the believer out from his hiding place in Christ, so he creates all kinds of commotion, symptoms, and devices to get him to peek outside that door.

In John 10:7, Jesus says, *"I am the DOOR OF THE SHEEP."*

When you receive Jesus as your Savior, you enter into a new world of blessing and provision. However, the only way is through the Door, Jesus. Go through that Door and don't come out, or you will be outside the blessings of God.

I know that as long as I stay hidden behind Jesus, He is my covering, and He blocks me from the enemy's view. I'm hidden!

When sickness tries to strike you, and the enemy roars with symptoms and pain, say, "No, Satan! I'm hidden in healing, and I'm not coming out!"

❦

FREE INDEED

"If the Son therefore shall make you free,
ye shall be free indeed."

John 8:36

Corrie ten Boom, a Christian woman from the Netherlands, was thrown into Nazi concentration camps during World War II for hiding Jews from the Nazis. The hiding of Jews was considered by the Nazis to be a crime punishable by death.

When first arrested, Miss ten Boom was repeatedly brought before a Nazi officer for interrogation regarding the whereabouts of the Jews she had been helping to hide.

She would give him no information, choosing to speak to him only about the salvation of his soul. Through the many times of interrogation, she gained favor with him, for she genuinely cared about him as a human being who was on his way to hell.

One day he took her into his office as usual. But this day he held in his hand all the documents Miss ten Boom had kept containing vital information about her family's operation of hiding Jews in their home.

The officer showed them to her and threatened, "Don't you know that these papers we have found seal your guilt and sentence you to death?"

She looked at him without a response.

He gathered all the papers in his hand, walked

over to the fireplace in his office, and cast them into the fire, destroying all the evidence against her.

That's what Jesus did for you and me.

> *...having forgiven you all trespasses; Blotting out the handwriting of ordinances that was against us, which was contrary to us, and took it out of the way, nailing it to his cross.*

Colossians 2:13, 14

All evidence of sin against you has been destroyed. No ordinances of your guilt of sin will ever hold up against you in the court of heaven if Jesus is your Lord. No past record of sin that Satan would try to recall could ever convict you, because Jesus has paid the price and canceled the debt you owed.

All those sins were nailed to His cross, the same cross that His blood flowed down, and that blood has washed them away. They exist no longer.

Has the remembrance of the past been a jail imprisoning your faith and keeping you from receiving what is rightfully yours?

If you have made Jesus your Lord, the sins you committed in your past don't exist any longer.

If you have committed sins since being born again, and their remembrance has paralyzed your faith, I John 1:9 tells us that if we confess our sins, God is faithful and just to forgive us of our sins. The cross did that for you and me.

Choose to be free from the past today, because healing awaits you!

PRAISING CONTINUALLY

"...His praise shall continually be in my mouth."
Psalm 34:1

We must come to realize that every time we talk about the tests, trials, or hardships we are going through, or we continually complain about physical problems, we are disobeying the above verse.

I cannot give God the praise due Him while magnifying or drawing attention to problems or tests I may be going through. How insulting to God to speak praises to Him one moment, then speak of the bigness of our problem the next!

If we would discipline our thoughts and words to praising God with gratitude, the power of that problem would grow small in comparison to His greatness, and the situation would cease to hold sway over us.

One of the most inspiring testimonies told about this principle is that of a young traveling minister who was diagnosed with tuberculosis in the mid-1900s.

As this minister traveled, he gave the doctor's report in every church he visited, and he requested each congregation to pray for him daily. The people all agreed to pray for his healing.

The disease, however, advanced until he was finally on his death bed at the home of his in-laws. One day he knew that death was near. As he looked out his bedroom window, a grove of trees in the distance caught his attention.

For some reason, he desired to go lay down among the trees. Although he was completely bedridden, he asked the Lord to give him strength enough to make it to the trees. After much time and effort, he arrived at the grove of trees and fell exhausted to the ground.

He lay there for a while. Then he began to think, "If it was prayer I needed to be healed, I would have been healed by now, because thousands of church members across the nation have agreed to pray for me daily. Prayer must not be what I am lacking."

He began talking to God, saying, "God, I'm just going to lie here and praise You until I'm either dead or healed!"

In his utter weakness, all he could do was faintly whisper, "I praise You, Lord. You're my Healer. Many great men of faith have laid hands on me and prayed for me, so according to your Word, I'm healed. Thank You that I'm healed now. Thank You, Lord!"

The young minister praised God like this for some time. At the end of about 30 minutes, he was able to lift up both hands. Then he received strength to talk in a normal speaking voice; and at the end of two and a half hours, he was standing on his feet, shouting praises to God so loudly that neighbors from miles around heard him. He was raised up completely well!

You will never come out of any bondage by continually talking about that bondage. That only holds you in it. Yet some people are in the habit of thinking and talking so much about their problems, they don't realize that is all they talk about!

When I call people on the phone, often the first thing out of their mouth is how sick they or their family are. That's just their habit — declaring the evil report; talking about how bad things are.

Why do they do that? They have not renewed their mind with the Word of God. No matter how much of the Bible you can quote, if the Word has not changed your conversation, it's because you haven't allowed it to change your way of thinking. Therefore, the Word is not in you. Yes, it may be in your memory, but it is not in your heart.

The Bible repeatedly tells us to meditate (mutter to ourselves, think deeply into) in the Word of God. Notice the Bible never uses the word "memorize." Memorization only affects the mind, but meditation affects the spirit — and you can only live on a daily basis out of what is in your spirit or heart.

That which is in your spirit will affect your mind, so feed your spirit daily through meditating on the Word of God. Allow the Spirit of God to help you in this area, because that is what He was sent to do for us.

The best way to silence the mind and give voice to your spirit is to keep the praises of God flowing continually from your heart. If you are alone, voice the praises with your mouth; and if you are surrounded by others, commune with the Lord quietly in your heart.

Whatever comes your way, speaking the praises of God from your heart on a continual basis are the wings that will cause you to "mount up" and live above life's difficulties and trials.

"...His praise shall CONTINUALLY be in my mouth."

KEEPING POWER

"(We) *are KEPT BY THE POWER of God through faith...*"
I Peter 1:5

When Daniel was cast into the lion's den, he experienced the power of God. When the Israelites were wandering through the wilderness, they lived with God's power. When the three Hebrew men were thrown into the fiery furnace, this power changed the fire. And for a moment, Peter partook of this power when he walked with Jesus on the water.

What power am I referring to?

It's the "keeping power" of God!

No matter what comes my way, I rely on that power to "keep" me. When others partake of the flu epidemic, I'm kept. When others fall into financial ruin, I'm kept. It has nothing to do with me — it's God's "keeping power"!

Believers know too little about this "keeping power" of God.

If we would learn to draw on His "keeping power," we wouldn't need to draw so often upon His "healing power" or His "miracle power." His "keeping power" is a higher way of living.

After I receive the power that heals me, I must depend on his "keeping power" to live healed.

This is why so many believers lose their healings. They don't realize that it takes power to live healed, just as it takes power to have healing manifested.

How do you obtain this "keeping power"?

I Peter 1:5 tells us, "(We) *are kept by the power of God THROUGH FAITH."*

As with everything else in the kingdom of God, faith is what activates God's "keeping power."

Let your conversations be filled with how dependent you are upon God's "keeping power" that is in you and around you. Then you won't live from crisis to crisis; you will live from power to power!

PRESSED INTO HIM

*Let the pressures of life press you into Him
instead of away from Him.*

In II Corinthians 1:8, Paul writes, *"...we were
PRESSED out of measure, above strength...."* The pressures
of life come to everyone, taking on different shapes
and forms, but pressures just the same.

For those who have allowed their daily fellowship
and abiding in God to grow distant, those pressures
succeed in only pushing many further away from Him.
But the ones who are abiding in God count it all joy
when the pressures, tests, and trials come their way, for
they see it as an opportunity to be pressed further into
the image of Christ, for Christ to be formed in them.

They have learned like James to:

> *Consider it wholly joyful, my brethren, whenever
> you are enveloped in or encounter trials of any
> sort, or fall into various temptations. Be assured
> and understand that the trial and proving of
> your faith bring out endurance and steadfastness
> and patience. But let endurance and steadfast-
> ness and patience have full play and do a thor-
> ough work, SO THAT YOU MAY BE [PEO-
> PLE] PERFECTLY AND FULLY DEVELOPED
> [WITH NO DEFECTS], LACKING IN NOTH-
> ING.*

James 1:2-4 (The Amplified Bible)

Learn to look at the tests and trials that come your way as you are instructed to see them by the Word of God, seeing them as perfecting in you those things that will never be perfected in you except through tests and trials.

Satan sends tests and trials our way in hope of destroying the faith in our hearts, but those abiding in God realize their faith is for the battle; we are not to lay down our faith in the midst of a test and run.

Decide to be stronger because of that test by learning to yield to the strength of God that's in you.

Decide to see God at every rock; then even the rocks will bless you. Decide to see God at every hard place; then even the hard places will bless you.

Don't let bitterness, unforgiveness, unbelief, or resentment come between you and Jesus, or the pressures of life will only succeed in pressing you further into them. But by keeping your heart pure and free from anything unholy, the pressures of life will only succeed in pressing you further into Him.

Then we can say with Paul the apostle, *"For me to live is Christ...."*

Day 13

❦

PRESS ON!

Press on!
Jesus is just within the press — waiting for you there!

> *And a certain woman, which had an issue of blood twelve years, and had suffered many things of many physicians, and had spent all that she had, and was nothing bettered, but rather grew worse, when she had heard of Jesus, CAME IN THE PRESS behind, and touched his garment. For she said, If I may touch but his clothes, I shall be whole. And straightway the fountain of her blood was dried up; and she felt in her body that she was healed of that plague.*
>
> Mark 5:25-29

The woman saw Jesus, but she needed more — she needed to touch Him. Only one thing stopped her: a "press."

How many times our answer is in sight, but it is unreachable because of the "press"!

For this woman, the "press" was the people she visibly saw. But there was also an unseen "press" against her.

She was in public around other citizens, which was strictly prohibited. According to Jewish Law, because of her flow of blood, she was considered unclean, and she would have been punished if found — yet she pressed on!

27

Every doctor she had seen during the past 12 years told her there was no hope for her. Yet when she saw Jesus, she chose to "press" beyond her doctors' reports, for she had heard the report about Another!

For twelve long years this condition had been in her body. She had to "press" beyond the mental visions of never being well again. (Never "get used to" symptoms.)

For twelve years she had steadily grown worse. What made her think this was the day that process would be reversed? She had to "press" beyond the knowledge of her daily declining health.

She had spent all her money on medical help that did not avail for her. She was a penniless woman "pressing" on.

Pain had become the norm for her. She was a suffering woman, and medical treatments had only accelerated her condition. Yet she could not allow her suffering to "press" her out of her healing.

Thoughts of doubt and unbelief undoubtedly waged war against her, making her mind wonder what difference the touch of a garment would make in her body; nevertheless, she still "pressed" on.

Once Jesus was in her view, the "press" was hardly noticeable! Keep Jesus before your eyes, and the "press" won't be as noticeable to you, either.

She had finally made it through! She touched Jesus' garment. Jesus knew in Himself that power had gone out of Him, and He *"...turned him about in the press..."* and asked who had touched Him.

Think of it! He could feel her touch even in the midst of the "press."

And she *"...came and fell down before him..."* She had made it through the "press"!

It is a "press" to get through the doubts, thoughts, circumstances, opinions, and symptoms, but don't fear the "press" — Jesus waits for you there!

ಳ

PRAY THE WORD

*Many believers are defeated and sick
because they pray demon-inspired prayers.*

Often, in listening to believers make their confes-
sions to God and say their prayers, I have heard dis-
turbing things. I have heard people who have had
automobile accidents in the past say, "I bind any car
accident from happening that the devil might have set
up for me."

Why do they pray that way? They are afraid of
another accident.

I have heard believers say, "I pray against any
tragedies happening to my family." Why would they
pray that way? Because they are afraid of tragedy strik-
ing their family. Satan has suggested that to their
minds, and they believe it, whether they know it or not.

I have heard a person call out diseases and sicknesses they don't even have, praying against them,
binding them from coming upon their bodies. Why
do they single out a particular sickness and pray
against getting it? Because they are afraid of it. They
have filled their ears and minds with all the latest evil
reports from the media, and they have become fearful.

That kind of praying ends up driving the fear
deeper into their hearts and minds.

Where do those fears come from? They come
from thoughts the enemy gives. These are what could

be called demon-inspired prayers or fear-dominated prayers.

This is the way Job prayed — fearful praying — and those fears, spoken under the guise of prayer, are what came upon him!

Prayers spoken in fear are nothing more than a red flag you wave at the devil, letting him know you heard him and believe him!

Fearful thoughts come to all, but you must resist them by telling those thoughts to flee, not by praying about them. If you pray a fearful thought, you have taken it as your own; but if you rebuke it, you have sent it back to the devil, where it came from. *"Resist the devil, and he will flee from you!"*

Examine your prayers and your words before you speak them to see what is motivating them.

When Satan puts a thought of fear in your mind about a sickness, accident, or tragedy, and you take that thought and begin praying against it, Satan's plan worked! He got you praying his thoughts!

They aren't really prayers at all; they are words of fear, spoken under the guise of prayer, and when you release them through words, you give those things an entrance into your life.

Satan desires those things to happen to you, but he's got to get you working with him in order to get them to come to pass. How does he do this? He infiltrates your prayer life through your thoughts, getting you to "pray against" fearful things. He is very deceiving, isn't he?

Never pray fearful thoughts. Always pray the Word!

If the thought is suggested to your mind, "I am going to hurt one of your children," do not pray, "Oh Lord, don't let anything hurt my children." That prayer shows that you believe the threats of Satan. He is not only guiding your thoughts, but your prayers as well. Satan has managed to get you to repeat the fear he suggested.

So never repeat the fear that Satan has suggested to your mind in your prayers to God.

Always pray the Word. All you need to say is, "I thank You, Father, that no weapon formed against the righteousness of God, my family and me, will prosper."

Your prayer now agrees with God's Word instead of Satan's thoughts. Do you see the fine line of deception?

Never single out a sickness or a disease you don't have and pray against it. That shows you are afraid of it, and the harder you pray, the more you will fear it; and it will come upon you, just as Job's prayers of fear came upon him.

Your prayer should be, "Himself took my infirmities and bare my sickness, and the number of my days will he fulfill."

It is the Word and the Word alone that rebukes Satan, not your fearful words of rebuke.

Remember, in the wilderness, Jesus always rebuked Satan by speaking the Word. He never repeated the temptation Satan spoke! (See Luke 4)

Always agree with the Word by praying the Word. Never repeat in prayer what Satan or fears suggest to your mind. If you do, you will be agreeing with Satan and those fears.

Don't pray, "I come against tragedies. They will not happen to this family." The person who prays that will be covering himself and his family with the power of a tragedy instead of the power of the Word!

Your prayer should be, "I have overcome Satan through the blood of the Lamb, and my testimony is about the power of the blood. That power covers me and my family now."

By praying the Word, you throw the focus of your thoughts and heart to the Word and away from fear.

You can have a correct confession, but if your prayers are demon-inspired and fear-motivated, they will dominate your life.

What if you have been praying the wrong way? What if you have been praying fearful words? Realize that you have been deceived. Repent and change today. Begin to speak only the Word over your life and the lives of your family and friends.

Agree with the Word, pray the Word, and trust the Word. Satan can never deceive or defeat the Word!

❧

SPEAK NO GUILE

"For he that will love life, and see good days,
let him refrain (hold back) *his tongue from evil,*
and his lips that they speak no guile."

I Peter 3:10

We like to believe that Satan is always the source of our problems in life, but the truth is, evil speaking fills a life with horrible things.

It is to be understood that Satan is the author of all sickness and evil, but the words we have spoken have sent an invitation to Satan to occupy our lives with hellish things.

The media and the world system are placing a major emphasis on the diet of this generation, but my Bible points out that one of the top killers of man is his tongue and not just his diet!

Christians are slow to change the way they use their tongues, because they are slow to change. It takes real change in the lives and hearts of believers for their tongues to show evidence of the change.

Why are we so slow to change what we say? Because we think too highly of what we say! We think we're always right. But Paul warns us in Romans 12:3 not to think more highly of ourselves than we ought.

Some people speak evil out of pure habit. Criticism and judging have become their way of thinking and speaking. They don't even listen to themselves anymore to notice how unbecoming they sound.

Are people safe with you when they're absent?

It takes a real effort to allow only sweet waters to flow from the tongue, but ask the Holy Spirit to help you, for He is the Helper! In fact, speaking only sweet words will help you achieve and maintain divine health!

Day 16

❦

RIVERS OF LIVING WATER

"...I will fear no evil: for thou art with me..."
Psalm 23:4

Because Satan is called "the god of this world," the currents of his evil and his forces are continually flowing around us (II Corinthians 4:4).

David wrote in Psalm 23, *"...in the presence of mine enemies..."* and *"...though I walk through the valley of the shadow of death..."* illustrating to us that the Earth is now a valley of death's shadows, and it is filled with our enemies and the currents of evil powers.

Those evil currents flow around us all the time, but take courage — another river is flowing! *"Out of* (your) *belly shall flow RIVERS OF LIVING WATER."* These rivers carry the currents of healing, peace, joy, prosperity, and all of God's other blessings.

If we are not full of His Spirit, through which these blessed rivers flow, we can become engulfed in the evil waters of Satan's currents that flow all around us.

In living this life of faith, we are constantly withstanding "the powers that be." It takes a constant stand of faith to yield to God's flow in a world whose established flow is evil.

A life lived in God is a life that continually fights the flow of the evil current; but don't become fearful or disheartened by that evil flow — just let the current of God's rivers cut a path through the enemy's chaotic flow and carry you past every obstacle.

Let God's rivers flow out of you, and they will do the work!

❧

KEEPING THE VICTORY

***Just because you can see the Egyptians
doesn't mean you're back in Egypt!***

When God brought the Israelites out of Egypt after 400 years of harsh bondage, they left that land behind and headed for the Promised Land.

Pharaoh is a type of Satan himself, the god of this world.

Egypt is a type of the world, with its many hardships and hard taskmasters, such as sickness, pain, disease, lack, torment, doubt, fear, unbelief, addictions, and poverty.

The Israelites are representative of God's people today.

The Promised Land is a type of the many blessings of God that belong to us, including healing, prosperity, peace, joy, and the baptism of the Holy Ghost.

When the Israelites were delivered from the land of Egypt and all that was harmful to them, notice the Egyptians tried to follow them into the Promised Land. They hotly pursued them with a large army. God's people in their own strength were defenseless against such an onslaught.

This is still the tactic the enemy uses today. Although we are free, he still pursues us and tries to bring the curses of Egypt into our Promised Land.

However, once you have been born again, you are

delivered from the Egyptian land of bondage. Colossians 1:13 states, *"[God] hath delivered us from the power of darkness, and hath TRANSLATED us into the kingdom of his dear Son."*

We didn't have to pack up and move to the Promised Land like the Israelites did; we were "translated" into it! That's much quicker! No 40 years of wandering through the wilderness for us.

Our only job is to stay on the right side of the Jordan River, not leaving the Promised Land to wander in the wilderness. We need only remain in the land of translation.

As in the days of the Israelites, those Egyptian taskmasters of sickness, disease, pain, and symptoms want to follow us, trying to make us believe we still belong to them as slaves. In our own strength and defenses, we are just as helpless as the Israelites were that day, but God is still as strong, mighty, and victorious as *He* was that day.

The Israelites were tempted to doubt that their new-found freedom would be long lived, but one man, Moses, dared to stretch out a rod of God's power and divide impassable waters.

Psalm 77:19, 20 reads, *"Thy way is in the sea, and thy path in the great waters, and thy footsteps are not known. Thou leddest thy people like a flock by the hand of Moses and Aaron."*

There was no need for God's people to fear the great sea that lay in front of them, because God had already walked that way ahead of them; the waters covered His footsteps. It wasn't until God divided the sea in front of them that they were able to see the path of God's steps.

God's path is not always the most obvious one, but it can easily be found if we will use our faith to divide and drive back that which seeks to keep His steps and His will hidden. However, God's path would never have been revealed if Moses had not dared to believe and act!

> ...*(taking paths which HE PREPARED AHEAD OF TIME), that we should walk in them [living the good life which he PREARRANGED and MADE READY for us to live].*
>
> Ephesians 2:10 (The Amplified Bible)

How many times had Moses seen the sea divide before? None! Real faith believes God will do something for you that you have never seen Him do for anyone else! Having seen it done previously is not the prerequisite for believing and acting.

Never be afraid to walk where God leads, for He has already been there and prepared the way, but He demands faith to cause His invisible footsteps to become visible to man.

When the Israelites saw the Egyptians seeking to overtake them, it did not mean they were back in Egypt, and it did not mean they still belonged to the Egyptians, because He whom the Son sets free is free indeed (John 8:36).

No curse of this world has legal right to be on you. Don't allow any pursuing Egyptians to convince you that you still belong to them. You were translated into freedom, and you are still free!

Believe that God has prepared a way before you. Stand on His promises, and drown those Egyptians in the water of the Word!

❦

CLOTHED WITH CHRIST

"But put ye on the Lord Jesus Christ..."

Romans 13:14

The Bible calls Satan *"the god of this world"* (II Corinthians 4:4). His forces all around us try to affect the inhabitants of this Earth in a negative way. Although believers are free from his bondage, we are not free from his attacks.

Attacks come against our bodies, because the forces of evil that surround us can be felt. Our bodies are subject to the attacks of these forces, but we are to be armed with spiritual armor that repels the attacks.

Astronauts have to be clothed in special space suits that permit them to leave their homeland of Earth and walk on other planets.

Even so, Earth is not my homeland. My homeland is a foursquare city in heaven! On planet Earth, I am surrounded by an atmosphere that is foreign to me and my true homeland. I am not naturally "suited" to this strange land.

Even to operate on this planet, I must be clothed in a special suit or special clothing that allows me to function here successfully. God has provided that clothing. We are to be *"clothed with Christ."* What a glorious covering He is for His children!

Nevertheless, Satan still tries to strip me of that clothing of Christ by trying to throw a cloak of pain and symptoms about me; but I put on *"the garment of praise"* that keeps my heavenly clothing unspotted and unsoiled by the attacks of the enemy.

So I don't consider my earthly body; I consider my heavenly covering!

Day 19

❦

STRANGERS
AND PILGRIMS

"...as he is, so are we in this world."

I John 4:17

The victory in this verse lies in having our eyes focused on Jesus Christ in *His* world instead of on us in *our* world. As Paul said in Ephesians 2:2, *"Wherein in time past ye walked according to the course of this world...."* The dictates of this world system are to be a thing of the past in our lives.

"...Old things are passed away; behold, all things are become new" (II Corinthians 5:17). Not only are we to see our old sin nature as a thing of the past in our lives, but this world system — which includes such things as sin, sickness pain, lack, unbelief, and torment — is no longer our system. We serve a higher government, which is the governing power of the Word of God.

Every country has a book of laws that governs the land, and heaven is no exception. Heaven is governed by its law book, the Word of God; and as citizens of that land, it is to govern our thoughts, bodies, homes, families, finances, and churches.

Upon receiving Jesus as your Savior, your citizenship was changed. Heaven is now your home, and your name is recorded in its roll book, the Book of Life, which is proof of your citizenship. That now makes you a stranger and a pilgrim in this world (Hebrews 11:13-16).

40

The ways of this world are to be foreign to you. They are not to be your ways any longer. No longer are you to seek to have your ways and manner of living mirror those of this world; your life is to exemplify Christ's life.

Jesus left His home in heaven, came to live in this world, yet lived with the order of heaven governing His life, ways, and actions, thereby teaching us by example how to live in this world while being governed by another world.

So, with the eye of faith I look into His realm, the Word of God, to see how He lived. Then I take those ways to myself and become like Him even while living in this world.

What do I see when I look at Him?

I see One raised from the dead, seated at the right hand of God in heavenly places, far above all principality, power, might, and dominion, with all things under His feet (Ephesians 1:20-22).

I see One who is ever praying for His Church, even as I must do before I can be like Him. I see Him who has utter joy, peace, rest, provision, wisdom, obedience, and health. To be like Him, these are the things I must possess and the things that must possess me.

To be like Him even while living in this world is not only my privilege and my right, but my responsibility.

Jesus is victorious and reigning. My victory is as long-lasting as His. I reign as long as He reigns. When this world has long passed away, my position remains the same, for I am in Him, and He is the same yesterday, today, and forever.

I look at His body and see no sickness, pain, or disease, and I say with my mouth, "As He is, so am I in this world."

THE EYE OF FAITH

*"While we look not at the things that are seen,
but at the things which are not seen..."*
II Corinthians 4:18

The things which are seen are ever trying to block our view of Him who is invisible. How, then, can we keep our eyes fixed on Him when all that would oppose Him is constantly trying to fill our vision?

There is only one way: Don't look!

The eye of faith has clearer vision than the human eye. It sees that which is far more sure and trustworthy than what the natural eye can ever look upon.

Faith's eye has the ability to see into the realm of God, where the view is heavenly; however, faith's vision gains clarity of focus only from the Word of God. The Word teaches us where to fix our gaze, and the Word brings clarity to the object of our focus, Jesus, the Unseen One.

Keep from seeing what this world tries to reveal by feeding on the Word of God until it captivates your total attention.

There are those skilled in the things of this world who give up to 18 hours a day to their professions. Can we give less than our all to be skillful in using the possessions heaven has bestowed upon its children?

We must learn to go about our daily duties while still seeing Him, living with an utter consciousness of

God and His presence. We are to see ourselves performing every daily task for His glory and honor. Then that task will become a way to worship Him. As the Bible says, "...whatsoever ye do, do all to the glory of God" (I Corinthians 10:31).

We cannot look at the seen things of this world to the glory of God. It glorifies Him when we see that which faith's eye reveals to us and focus all of our heart, thoughts, words, acts, and life upon it.

In fact, to look at what is seen is a sin against God. The job of the believer is to "look not" at what we see with our eyes or feel in our bodies.

The Weymouth translation of Hebrews 11:24-27 says Moses "...fixed his gaze on the coming reward. Through faith he left Egypt, not being frightened by the king's anger; for HE HELD ON HIS COURSE AS SEEING THE UNSEEN ONE."

You, too, will be held to your course of healing by seeing the unseen One.

Moses fixed his gaze on what was to come; not on what he had. If you will take your attention off the present condition of your body and put it on what you want to come to your body, that act will bring the manifestation of healing.

If you are born again, you have left Egypt, just as Moses did. You were delivered from the kingdom of darkness at the time of your new birth. The scripture tells us of Pharaoh's anger against Moses for leaving, but notice that Moses did not let that frighten him.

Satan is angry because you have been delivered from his kingdom, and he will try to manifest his anger through sickness, pain, and lack, but be as Moses — unafraid!

To look to God and His Word means to have your gaze completely riveted at all times, with your full attention upon Him only; and if that means you must sleep with your Bible in your arms to steady your gaze, so be it!

Stay on course, because your destination is in sight
— faith's sight, that is!

🍂

SOAKED IN THE WORD

After you have taken Jesus as the Healer of your body,
don't ever let the thought to check your body
for symptoms into your thought life.

Too often we are too body-conscious instead of Word-conscious. We say we take God's healing power into our bodies according to the Word; then we start to check our bodies to see if we're healed.

Healing flows from the Word, not from our bodies, so why would we check our bodies? We aren't healed according to our bodies; we are healed according to the Word! I'm healed because the Word says so, not because my body says so. So in checking your body, you're checking the wrong thing. Check the Word!

To check your body every day for healing would be the same as Moses and the Israelites traveling back into Egypt every day, checking to see if they were still free. Going back into the land of what you feel, hear, and see will throw you back into Egypt's slavery — sickness!

To walk in divine health, you must never listen to your body!

By walking with the Word and the Spirit as your guide, you will travel deeper into the Promised Land of health. By looking at and checking your body, you show that your attention is focused on something other than the Word, and that alone will defeat you.

You must be soaked and saturated in the healing Word daily to silence the human desire to be led by your body.

Your body is not the author of health. Therefore, don't look at your body, but be *"Looking unto Jesus the author and finisher..."* (Hebrews 12:2).

ༀ

ACTIVATING GOD'S POWER

God's power is present everywhere.
God is a healing God, so where He is, healing is!

In a vision when Jesus appeared to Kenneth E. Hagin, Jesus told him that God's power is present everywhere, and there is enough power in every sick room and in every hospital room to raise up that sick one. However, they remain as they are because they don't know that power is there, so they don't activate it.

The laws of electricity have been present since the time of Adam, but no one benefitted from electricity because no one knew of its presence. Benjamin Franklin gained knowledge of its presence, but it was Thomas A. Edison who began to experiment with components that could harness the power of electricity, conduct it, and channel it, thereby blessing humanity.

Likewise, God's power is present everywhere, but we must have knowledge of its presence before we can benefit from it. Edison had knowledge that electricity was present, but even then he had to learn how to conduct it.

To benefit from God's power that is everywhere present, you must learn how to conduct it! How? The Word of God is the manual that teaches us how to conduct that power.

Faith is the cable that links us to that power, and

the words of faith you speak "flip the switch" that causes the power to flow from the unseen realm to the
seen realm of your body.

We don't see electricity until we flip the electrical
switch on the wall. What was once unseen now enters
the seen realm through a lamp or other electrical
devices.

Often, in California, we see a child receiving as a
birthday gift a Mexican piñata, a colorful papier-
mache animal or other shape filled with candy and
treats. All the children at the birthday party are blind-
folded, and each takes a turn trying to hit the piñata,
which hangs from the ceiling. If a child hits the piñata just right, it breaks, and all the candy and treats fall
to the ground and the children gather them up.

Just because God's healing power is present
doesn't mean it's flowing. That power must be struck
for it to be released.

What kind of strike will release it? Talking about
the pain? Begging God to do something? No, faith
must strike that power for it to be released!

When my second son, Grant, was three weeks old,
it was found he had a temperature of 102 degrees.
The doctor immediately hospitalized him, because he
was so young to have such a high fever.

Nurses placed him in a room and prepared to run
several tests and give him medication, but they told me
it would be a while before someone would be in to give
him any treatment.

I just sat with him in a rocking chair. I didn't ask
anything of God; I only reminded Him what He had
told the prophet, Brother Hagin.

I said, "Jesus, You appeared to the prophet. I
believe that. You told him that God's power was present everywhere. I believe that. You told him that
God's power was in every sick room and in every hospital room, too. I believe that. I am not asking You for

anything other than what is already present.

"I believe in that power! I believe it's right here! I believe it surrounds me and my baby. But that's not enough — I want it to work in my baby's body. I want it to be released in his body.

"I realize it's my job to release it, and it's your job to see that it performs what it is released to do."

"So I say with my mouth, because I believe in my heart, that Your healing power is present to destroy the works of darkness. And with my faith I strike the power and say that it *now* flows into my baby's body and destroys sickness, symptoms, and pain, in Jesus' Name! Thank You for it. It is *now* at work in the body of my baby."

For the next hour I continued to thank God for the manifestation of that power in my baby's body. I envisioned that healing power as a heavenly substance flowing throughout his body.

The devil could have given me other imaginations of sickness and bad reports, but my imagination was already occupied with seeing God's healing power at work, so there was no vacancy for him.

At the end of that hour, the nurse returned to take his temperature once again, and she said it was completely normal. The baby had received no medication from the doctors. The presence of God's power put into action healed him. Hallelujah!

That same power is present right where you are, too. Recognize that power! Talk about that power, and it will be released to work in you!

Too many talk about the power of sickness. In doing so, they release that power to work in them. But God's power is greater, because *"Greater is He that is in you than he that is in the world."*

According as HIS DIVINE POWER HATH GIVEN unto us all things that pertain unto life

and godliness, THROUGH THE KNOWL-
EDGE of him...

II Peter 1:3

While lying in your bed at night, repeat it to your-self over and over again: "His power is in this very room. It flows into my body *now* and heals me!"

When fearful thoughts come to you in the night, start talking about that power, and continue to let it do its work. Healing power is present, so make your faith do its job — and let that power flow!

Day 23

❦

GOD'S MEDICINE

*"(God's words) are life unto those that find them,
and health (medicine) to all their flesh."*
Proverbs 4:22

While riding in the car one day, my son, Stephen, began to complain of a pain in his stomach. After questioning him, I learned that he had suffered with flare-ups of the condition for about two years, but he had never said anything about it.

I used the above scripture and explained it to him, saying, "Because the Word of God is medicine to our bodies, we must take the medicine and give it time to do its work."

I explained that when we prayed and agreed for his healing, it would work like any medicine that is taken. After you swallow that medicine, you don't see it anymore, but you can remember when you took it, and you know it must be in you, even though it is no longer visible.

"So when we pray," I explained, "the dose of the Word begins to work in your body. You won't see it working, but you can think back, remember when we prayed, and remember that is when the dose of God's medicine was taken. Just as natural medicine's power does its work in you, so the Word's power does its work in you."

Throughout the day, I would stop him and ask,

"What is working in you?"

"Healing power," he would reply.

Later I would question him again. "Where's that healing power working?"

"In my body," was his response.

At the end of three hours, every pain had left, and it has never returned.

Every time we talked about the power of the Word, we were taking another dose of God's medicine!

People will give a doctor's prescription weeks and months to do its work, but they will accuse God's Word of being unable to heal them after taking only one dose of the Word — diluted with doubt!

Give God's medicine the same opportunity you give man's medicine. Take it faithfully, daily, and as prescribed. It will do its work in you. Just give it time — and faith!

Day 24

❧

HIGHER THOUGHTS

"Take no thought for your life..."
Matthew 6:25

Too often we are defeated because of our thought life. Too many believers keep themselves bound by sickness because they are continually thinking about the sickness and their bodies.

Faith not only has a way of talking; faith also has a way of thinking.

Isn't it difficult to ignore your body when there is pain in it? Yes, but there is a way for it to be done. By giving your thoughts to the Word, thinking about what the Word says, the Word instead of your body will begin to control your thoughts. That's the way you "mount up with wings as eagles" and live above what your body is telling you.

Many are sick today because they have worried about their bodies. All they think about is their bodies. *"For to be carnally minded is death; but to be spiritually minded is life and peace"* (Romans 8:6).

Your mind will carry thoughts about your body unless you occupy your mind with the healing Word. You must learn to cast down *"...imaginations, and every high thing that exalteth itself against the knowledge of God..."* (II Corinthians 10:5).

The devil will fight you for your thoughts and your mind, but if you fill your thoughts with the Word of

God, the Word will do the fighting for you, and you will see that "...*the battle is the Lord's.*"

Every thought you allow in your mind is either a battle lost or a victory gained. Thoughts against the Word will come, but you must cast them down. To cast them down effectively, you must pick up other thoughts in their place — thoughts about the Word!

Isaiah tells us that God's thoughts are higher than our thoughts. To live above the thoughts of our bodies and this world and to come up to God's level, we must come up higher in our thought life.

Higher thoughts are the route to victory — they are the thoughts of the Word.

❦

THE HOUSE OF HEALING

"...by whose stripes ye were healed."

I Peter 2:24

One day while meditating on this verse, the Spirit of God gave me an illustration that blessed me immeasurably.

I had pain in my body and symptoms that were persisting, so as I meditated on this scripture, the Holy Spirit asked me a question: "If someone bought you a house, paid cash for it, and gave you the title deed to the house, telling you it was yours, would it be yours?"

"Yes," I replied.

"Even if you didn't move into it until five years after you were given the title deed, would it still be yours?" He questioned.

"Absolutely," I replied.

"When did you own it — when you were given the title deed to the house, or when you took possession of the house?"

"Well, I owned it when I received the title deed, long before I took possession of it."

Jesus has given you the title deed to the house of healing. Take possession of the healing that you have owned all along!

Healing was purchased for you when Jesus took those stripes upon His back, was crucified, and was then resurrected.

The Word of God is a legal copy of the title deed to the house of healing that Jesus has provided for you, so wait no longer, and move into the house that has been yours all along!

The Spirit of God made it so clear to me how an event that took place 2000 years ago is still at work today. Now I can say with revelation, "By His stripes I was healed!"

PAID IN FULL

Debt canceled! The bill has been paid in full!

Every person who has ever shopped knows what receipts are and what their purpose is. Most women use them as lining for their purses, while others use them for scratch pads, but no businessman or store was the first to give receipts — God was!

When we buy an item at the store, we are given a receipt as proof to anyone that the item has been paid for. If the purchased item is faulty, has defects, or has parts missing, we are assured of receiving a replacement if we return the item with the receipt.

The Old Testament records how God's people were delivered from Egyptian bondage. Later, they began to grumble and speak against God and His servant, Moses, because of the difficulty of their journey to the Promised Land.

Because the children of Israel displeased the Lord and spoke against Him and Moses, they left the will of God and thereby left the protection of God.

What the Israelites didn't realize was that serpents were plentiful in the wilderness; however, because the protection of God had been so all-encompassing, they never even knew all the dangers they were being protected from.

They didn't realize how dangerous it would be for them to be outside God's protection, so they spoke against God and Moses with no fear of doing so.

After moving out from under God's protection through their grumbling words, they moved into the territory of judgment. Deadly, fiery serpents infiltrated their camp. Thousands of Israelites died and became ill from the serpents' bites.

The children of Israel repented to God and Moses. Then God gave them instructions on how to be healed. He told them to make a fiery serpent and set it upon a pole, and everyone who looked upon the pole would be healed.

There was healing power on the serpent on that pole, because it was a type of Jesus Christ hanging on the cross for the sins and sicknesses of humanity! What released that healing power?

Their look!

According to Numbers 21:8, *"...every one that is bitten, when he LOOKETH upon it, shall live."* Notice, if they had gazed in a direction other than the pole, healing would not have been theirs.

The direction you look determines the direction you will go!

Looking unto Jesus means more than a glance at the Word during the Sunday morning service. It means a continual feeding and constant dependence on the Word. Steady your gaze. It must be intent and immovable!

Those Israelites received healing that day by looking at just the foreshadow of Christ. How much more readily is healing available to the one who looks to Christ Himself and not merely a shadow of Him, as the Israelites did.

They received healing on credit that day. Then, at Calvary, the bill was stamped "paid in full"!

The healing scriptures are receipts for you and me to carry with us to show Satan that the bill of sickness and disease has been paid and canceled.

Suppose you owed a bill at the grocery store and went in one day to pay it, but before you could reach the counter, a friend met you and said, "Don't bother to pay your bill. I have already paid it, and here's the receipt as proof it has been paid." You would thank him and take the receipt.

If the owner approached you and said, "You still owe me for the bill you ran up," you would respond, "Oh no. I have a receipt right here showing that my friend paid my bill in full. You can't charge me twice."

Healing scriptures are our receipts showing that the debt we owed has been canceled. Jesus, the Friend who sticks closer than a brother, is the One who paid our debts!

So when the devil brings symptoms and pains around you, trying to collect on the same bill twice, you just tell him, "No! That debt has been paid in full, and this Bible is my receipt, showing the debt was paid on Calvary!"

Day 27

༈

THE LAST APOSTLE

"Jesus Christ the same yesterday, and to day, and forever."
Hebrews 13:8

Some preachers and denominations have believed, preached, and taught that healing and miracles were done away with when the last of Jesus' apostles died.

I must relay a story to you that I heard another minister tell.

He was raised in a denomination that taught that healing and miracles passed away when the last apostle died. He tells of sitting in a service one night after he had entered the ministry. As he was listening to the preacher, he began thinking about the wrong doctrine that denomination had taught him all his life about healing.

He had since learned from the Word of God that healing and miracles are for today, and he currently has a strong healing ministry.

While he was thinking of all this, God gave him a vision. In the vision, a large screen appeared before him, and he watched these words appear on it: "HEALING AND MIRACLES PASSED AWAY WHEN THE LAST APOSTLE DIED."

The minister was shocked, because he knew the Word of God teaches differently. Then the rest of the vision appeared on the screen: "BUT THE LAST APOSTLE ISN'T DEAD YET!"

59

Jesus said, "...*I am the first and the last*" (Revelation 1:17). As long as the believer lives on the Earth, there will be healings and miracles, because Jesus is the Healer, and He abides forever!

You won't be healed just because Jesus is the Healer; you will be healed because you believe Jesus is *your* Healer. He can only be to you what you believe Him to be.

Day 28

❧

A PACKAGE DEAL

I am the healed!

Too often we find ourselves trying to grasp at faith or healing. This throws us into a panic and into the mental arena instead of the arena of faith.

When I was born again in 1979, receiving eternal life, I also received the benefits of that eternal life — health, prosperity, joy, peace, and all of God's blessings — so I am just as much healed as I am saved. They are a "package deal."

If the temptation to sin comes to me, I am still saved, but sin is trying to steal my salvation. I don't have to grasp for my salvation; I am already saved. I just protect my salvation by resisting.

In the same way, symptoms may try to come to me to steal my health, but that doesn't mean I am no longer "the healed." I am "the healed" just like I'm "the saved!" I don't have to grasp for healing. I am healed. I am just to resist that which tries to steal it.

Satan wants us to grasp for healing, because that act causes us to begin to question whether we have healing. He wants us to question our position in God instead of resisting him and his works.

Someone may say, "Well, I don't feel healed."

Healing isn't a feeling; it's a position.

I am healed because of my position in Christ, not because of the feelings in my body. Likewise, I am saved because of my position in Christ, not because I feel I'm saved.

I am seated with Him in heavenly places. Victory can't help but be mine. My position demands it!

61

❦

IN THE
FIERY FURNACE

Don't let the fire change your confession.
Make your confession change the fire!

One of my favorite Bible stories is the one in Daniel that tells of Shadrach, Meshach and Abednego being thrown into the fiery furnace.

King Nebuchadnezzar warned them to fall down like every other leader in the kingdom and worship his golden image. Of course, these three Israelites refused. They declared boldly that their God would deliver them from the burning, fiery furnace.

Nebuchadnezzar thought this was no way to talk to a king, so he had the furnace heated seven times hotter than before! The Jews' bold confession scared him so badly, he thought they could be right, so he had the heat in the furnace increased to ensure they would be burned up.

Have you ever noticed when symptoms appear and you boldly proclaim the Word of God resisting them, they sometimes increase like this fiery furnace? That only means that your bold believing has scared the enemy, so he's trying to frighten you.

Notice that the three Hebrews didn't change their confession just because the fire changed. Don't change your confession when the symptoms change in your body. Even if they do increase, faith still operates the same, so don't change your stand.

There is one thing that cannot be overlooked about these three young friends of Daniel: Their words and their faith agreed with each other and with God.

If you are walking through a fiery test, you cannot afford to surround yourself with companions who are speaking words of doubt every time you speak words of faith.

These three godly men had the same testimony — victory!

Jesus — the Fourth Man — was in the fire with them, and the fire had to change!

After they walked unharmed out of the fiery furnace, the leaders of Babylon gathered that day and saw *"...these men, upon whose bodies the fire had no power..."* (Daniel 3:27).

Make that confession yours: "The fire has no power upon my body!"

Day 30

❧

POWERLESS
SHOUTS

*Words of doubt and shouts of victory
from the same mouth are powerless!*

When the Israelites were directed by God to march
around the walls of Jericho, their instructions were to
look straight ahead, and keep their mouths shut! (See
Joshua 6:10.)

That in itself is the best thing for every believer to
learn: look straight ahead at Jesus, and keep your
mouth shut to words of doubt, unbelief, and evil
speaking.

When you do that, your shout of victory will be
effective. A shout that is preceded by days of wandering eyes and unbelieving words will fall flat to the
ground, leaving the walls standing strong and intact!

Just because a person shouts in church louder than
anyone else doesn't mean much; especially when there
are walls still standing all around him in his own life.

If you are shouting victory, and the walls are still
up, check to see if your eyes are completely focused on
Jesus and your mouth is shut to doubt, unbelief, and
evil speaking.

Words of doubt and shouts of victory from the
same mouth will never work! Bitter and sweet waters
will never flow from the same fountain.

Healing manifests more quickly in those who live
their lives with their gaze fixed daily on Jesus and their

mouths guarded from all evil speaking. All that remains for them to do to obtain victory is the shout!

Those, however, who only want to shout will prolong their manifested healing until they steady their gaze and guard their mouths.

When the walls of Jericho fell, the shout was only a small part of the miracle that caused them to collapse. The miracle began days before, while the walls were still up. A fixed gaze, a guarded mouth — and THEN a shout!

CALLING THE INVISIBLE

Faith "calls" the invisible into the visible realm.

Because Jesus commands us to believe we *have received* the things we pray for at the time we pray and before they take visible form, it is clear that the answer exists in two forms: First, in the invisible form; and, second, in the visible form.

We must believe we *have received* our answers in their invisible form before we will see them in their visible form.

Our home sits on two and a half acres of land, but it is surrounded by many acres of undeveloped land. There are hills, ditches, roads, and bushes that have been personally inspected by our son, Stephen.

Sometimes in his exploring, Stephen will wander pretty far from the house, and I can't see him. But if it's time to eat and I call long enough and hard enough, no matter where he is, he comes running.

I call Stephen even though I don't see him at the time, because I know I have a Stephen. I know he belongs to me, and if I call long enough and loud enough, I will see him.

In the same respect, I may not see healing in my body, but I call my body healed because I know healing belongs to me, and if I continue to call, it will show up. I know healing exists; it's waiting for my faith to call it from its invisible form.

Faith sees the invisible healing and calls it, because faith knows it exists in the invisible realm. By calling it in faith, I transfer it from the invisible realm to the visible realm.

The first chapter of Genesis tells us that in the beginning, the Earth was dark. God is light, and there is light in His realm, but in the realm of the Earth, there was no light.

God wanted to bring what was in His realm to the realm of Earth. He wanted to make a transfer from the invisible realm to the visible realm. How did He do it?

He said, *"...Let there be light: and there was light."*

God made transfers from His realm to this realm through words; but not just empty words — faith-filled words!

How did He know it would work?

He knew light already existed in His realm, so He had no problem believing He could cause it to exist in this realm.

We won't have problems with our faith when we realize that health exists in God's realm, because there is no sickness in heaven. Believing it already exists there, we can boldly speak words of faith, knowing that is what causes the transfer.

You cause the invisible to become visible with your words!

❦

LEAVING THE SENSE REALM

To walk in faith means you have left the sense realm.

This world we live in is a world that trains the five physical senses and lives off the information gathered from them.

The realm of God, on the other hand, operates outside the five physical senses. To operate successfully in the realm of God, we must live above the confines of our five senses.

Our five physical senses aren't wrong; they are just confined to this earthly realm and are thus unable to perceive the knowledge that God's realm gives us.

Faith is the conductor receiving the knowledge that God's realm gives, but too many people try to conduct God's power through the five physical senses — and fail. Then they accuse that "faith stuff" of not working.

They weren't working in the realm of faith, or it would have worked. They were still in the sense-realm and mistakenly called it faith.

The five physical senses aren't the proper conductor for God's power — faith is! You've got to be wired right! That would be just like an electrician trying to wire a house with plastic, then hollering that electricity doesn't work. Oh yes, electricity works! You're just not wired right.

People who holler that faith doesn't work aren't

bad people — they're just not wired right. The five physical senses can't conduct God's power; only faith can.

Why do people hold so strongly to their five physical senses? Because they are better acquainted and more familiar with them than they are with faith. As you become more familiar with the way faith operates, you will see that faith is a more sure way of living.

God seeks to manifest His realm into our realm, but He can only cause it to manifest through our faith; not through what we see, feel, and hear in this realm. We must see with eyes that see another realm and hear with ears that are alert to the voice of Another.

If you live limited by the five senses of this earthly realm, you are bound to receive only what this realm can give. However, if you make the choice to allow faith to guide your vision, the wealth of the kingdom will manifest for you and through you.

SPIRITUALLY DISCERNED

It doesn't have to be understood to be believed!

How can the death and resurrection of God's Son that occurred 2000 years ago cause me to go to heaven? I don't understand it, but I believe it!

How can my giving money away through tithes and offerings cause me to receive more? I don't understand it, but I believe it!

How can my confession of a healing scripture spoken over my body cause health to reign there? I don't understand it, but I believe it!

These blessings are all spiritual laws that were set in operation by God, and any spiritual law that is obeyed will work.

We can study God's Word and gain a level of understanding and insight into these laws of God; and although the natural mind cannot conceive or comprehend their operation, the spirit of man receives it simply because his spirit believes it, not just because he understands it.

Many fail to receive healing because they want to understand it's operation before they will choose to believe it. If that is their attitude, they will never walk in the fullness of God's blessing. The laws of God must be believed to be activated — not understood!

> *But the natural man receiveth not the things of the Spirit of God: for they are foolishness unto him: neither can he know them, because they are SPIRITUALLY DISCERNED.*

I Corinthians 2:14

Your natural mind does not have the capacity to

comprehend what your spirit is capable of believing. Hebrews 11:6 says, *"...he that cometh to God must BELIEVE...."* It doesn't say that he that cometh to God must understand.

Understanding has nothing to do with believing. Faith has to do with believing. Faith will believe what the mind doesn't understand.

If I boarded an airplane and told the pilot, "I refuse to fly on this aircraft unless I understand how it works," I would never fly anywhere. My mind has not been trained to comprehend all the technical terminology it would take for me to understand how a plane flies.

I get on that plane and fly clear across the country because I believe that a man I have never met knows more about flying than I do.

Why don't we give God the same honor?

Every day we commit our lives into the hands of people we have never met while they do tasks for us that we don't understand. Why do we do this? Because we believe in them.

We will follow the advice of a dentist and let him drill in our mouth, using techniques and instruments we don't understand.

We will allow the lives of our children to be guided by teachers we have seldom met, teaching them things we don't understand, because we believe in them.

Don't tell me your mind has to understand it before your heart believes it! And don't ever try to tell God that! He sees you cast your faith blindly upon perfect strangers every day.

How disappointing it must be to God when we demand proof of Him. We are to be quick to believe God instead of being quick to believe our bodies or the enemy.

It's the believing person who receives; not just the understanding person.

If it's in the Word — believe it!

71

❦

LIFE OR DEATH

"...Be careful what you are hearing..."
Mark 4:24 (The Amplified Bible)

It could mean life and death what church you go to!

One day a woman was telling me about a friend of hers who had died in middle age. She didn't understand it, and she said it would be one of the first things she would ask Jesus when she saw Him.

The Spirit of God spoke up in me and said, "She died because she attended the wrong church. Her church didn't believe in healing; therefore, this person wasn't healed."

People erroneously think that if healing was for them, and if God wanted them healed, healing would just "drop" on them. They didn't get saved with that kind of thinking; why would they get healed with that kind of thinking?

Before you were saved, someone had to tell you about salvation. Then you had to believe it and receive it.

It's the same with healing. For people to know that God wants them healed, they must read it in the Bible, or someone has to tell them. Then they must believe it to receive it. People can't believe something they don't know is available!

What if you sat in a church that taught God didn't

want you to go heaven, and He was sending you to hell? How would you ever receive salvation? You wouldn't!

How, then, can people sit in a church that teaches people that God made them sick or healing isn't for everyone? How would these people ever get healed in that church? They wouldn't!

God doesn't heal people just to prove He can heal anymore than He saves people just to prove He can save. People must believe!

But how can people believe for God to heal them when the preachers say that God made them sick or that healing isn't for everyone?

If your church doesn't believe and preach divine healing is for everyone every day, you had better get out of there before you die there! It is a serious matter.

Be careful what you are hearing! Make sure it's the Word of God you hear, because God sent His Word and healed them!

Day 35

❦

HOLD FAST

"WITH God all things are possible!"
Matthew 19:26

Too many Christians have left God and their position *with* God — the place where all possibilities lie. They live apart from God and then wonder what is wrong, accusing God of all kinds of injustice.

Although healing belongs to you as a believer, you must live close to God in order to obtain and keep it. *"WITH God all things are possible,"* but aside from God, impossibilities prevail. We must "hold fast" to this God whom we trust!

But that which YE HAVE already HOLD FAST till I come.

Revelation 2:25

We need more of God than anything else in our lives. When I was born again, He set up His kingdom in me. I don't have healing if I don't have God. I don't have peace if I don't have God. I don't have abundance if I don't have God.

We don't need more health; we need more of God. We don't need more money; we need more of God. We don't need more peace; we need more of God.

More of God brings more of these things. He is to be our great desire and longing.

Jesus told us He came so we might have life, and

74

have it *more abundantly*. This shows we can have *measures* of God's power and presence operating in and through us. Let's seek His fullness!

The enemy seeks to steal the things I have from me, even seeking to draw me away from my God. How do I stay with God in the midst of it all?

Hold fast!

The dictionary meaning of "hold" is to remain in a particular position. The meaning of "fast" is deep and undisturbed.

Therefore, we would be correct in saying that to "hold fast" in the life of the believer means to remain in victory's position, deep and undisturbed. The only place that is possible is with God. It's the position Christ purchased for us!

Have you ever noticed how the devil is always trying to disturb everything around you? Stay with God. The enemy can't disturb Him. There's nothing like being in the undisturbed position when the storms of life hit.

Hold fast to your position *with* God. It always has victory in its view — it's the view of possibility!

EXAMINE YOURSELF

"But let a man examine himself..."
I Corinthians 11:28

Once when going through an attack that came
against my body, I heard reports from others who told
me it would take years before the symptoms would sub-
side. I even knew of people who had suffered with this
condition for years, and they were still suffering from
it.

One of my greatest battles during this time was to
keep my eyes and ears off what I was seeing and hearing from the lives of these people who were suffering
from the same condition.

I asked the Holy Spirit, who is my Counselor, to
give me counsel as to how to keep my eyes from looking at those who were themselves struggling.

He made the words *"But let a man examine himself..."*
come alive to me. I saw that it was a sin against God
and His Word to ever consider the physical condition
of another person or to compare my physical condition with that of another.

My God-given Bible rights give me permission to
examine only myself. (Try this truth in your marriage,
too. You will be amazed to discover that imperfections
don't reign only in the life of your spouse!)

The Holy Spirit then graciously asked me this question: "Do you ever look at your neighbor's checkbook
to see if you can pay your bills?"

"Why, of course not!" was my response.

"Then why," He continued, "do you look at someone else's body to see if *you* are healed?"

Needless to say, I got the message!

Day 37

❧

IMPERFECT RESULTS

If you've done all you know to do and you're still not healed, it's because you don't know enough.

When healing doesn't come as quickly as some think it should, believers must be careful not to accuse God in their comments, implying that He isn't "holding up His end of the bargain."

Imperfect knowledge always obtains imperfect results.

If you are not perfectly healed, your knowledge of healing is the first place to examine.

If there is any changing that needs to be done, get started, because you're the only candidate elected to change. God doesn't change. Why should He? Since He's perfect, change isn't in His agenda!

77

Day 38

❦

DOUBTFUL THOUGHTS

I am not moved by what I see. I am not moved by what I feel. I am moved only by what I believe.

What you see has great ability to move you. What you feel carries equal ability. But what you believe is greater. What you believe has the ability to change what you see and feel.

If you are born again, you are a believer. Believing is part of your spiritual nature. Give yourself to what you believe instead of to what you feel and see.

Often, people think they don't believe because doubts come to their minds. It doesn't mean you don't believe in your heart when doubts come to your mind. You've just got to make a decision to side with what you believe in your heart and not to side with the doubts in your mind.

Faith in your heart will work even when there are doubts in your mind.

Even if the battle in your mind is great, speak what you believe in your heart, and it will dominate and diminish the power of those thoughts in your mind.

Faith, when acted upon, is more powerful than opposing thoughts. As you operate with your faith instead of those doubtful thoughts, they will bow to your faith, and your faith will obtain the victory!

78

❦

THE POWER
OF THE BLOOD

"They overcame him (Satan) *by the blood of the Lamb, and
by the word of their testimony…"*

Revelation 12:11

This verse reveals to us that the blood of Jesus
always overcomes Satan and his works. But this verse
also tells us that for the blood of Jesus to do its work,
we have to add our testimony to that blood. What
does that mean?

We must testify with our mouths that the blood of
Jesus does overcome all the power of the enemy. We
must declare that the power of Jesus' blood is greater
than all other power and believe now that it overcomes
all evil, regardless of what we see and feel.

When sickness, symptoms, doubt, unbelief or any
other evil tries to attach itself to us, we are to fill our
mouth with the testimony of how Jesus' blood defeats
that evil which attacks us. We tell the enemy that the
evil cannot stay because the blood is greater and does
overcome. We are to hold onto that confession, contin-
uing to declare it until all the evil leaves us.

When the Israelites were delivered from the cen-
turies of slavery under the Egyptians, blood played a
major role in their deliverance.

A spirit of death from hell traveled through the
land of the Egyptians to slay the firstborn of every
household. But God's people, the Israelites, were

promised safety. They were to take the blood of a flaw-less lamb and spread it on the doorpost of their home. When the spirit of death traveled through the land, that blood on their doorpost forbade entrance of that evil and God's people were held in safety, in the hiding place provided by the blood.

The blood of that slain lamb was a type of Christ, the perfect Lamb. His blood was shed for us and it still flows freely today, so we have continuous access to it. We don't take actual blood and spread it as the Israelites did, we spread the blood of Jesus over our lives by the words we say and by believing that it takes place as we say those words. By our words we confess that we have our freedom from all evil and that the blood brings victory to pass.

But the Israelites didn't just stop by spreading the blood of the lamb on their doorpost. They were instructed by God to take the body of that lamb and eat it, leaving none uneaten.

So we too are not to stop at just speaking the power of the blood over our lives, but we are to also take the body of the Lamb and to eat it. The Bible tells us that the Word, Jesus, became flesh and dwelt among us. So the body of the Lamb that we are to eat and continuously feed upon is the Word of God.

To gain complete victory, we must speak of the all-conquering power of the blood of Jesus and continu-ously feed upon the Word of God, leaving none of it uneaten.

Satan cannot ever change the blood of Jesus or the power that is in the blood of Jesus, so he tries to get us to change our testimony about the blood. Our testi-mony is the only variable in this case. If we cease to say that the blood is our victory, it will cease to do its work for us. If the enemy can get you to think that it doesn't do its work because you may not see immedi-ate results, he will change your testimony about the blood, thereby stopping its power from flowing for you.

Jesus said, *"This . . . is the new testament in my blood."* In other words, all that belongs to you and all the promises of the new testament come to you through the power of the blood. Nothing of the new testament can come to you except through the blood.

Increase your testimony about the power of the blood in your life. Don't let a day go by that you don't talk about the power of the blood of Jesus to do it's victorious work in your life. Talk about the power of the blood, think about the power of the blood, believe in the power of the blood.

It's not you who have to overcome the enemy. Get your eyes off of you and your own inabilities. In your own self, your own power or your own ability, you could never defeat the enemy. God knows that, that's why He sent His Son to obtain your victory. Keep your eyes on Jesus and keep your testimony on the power of His blood to obtain the victory and the blood will do its all-conquering work in your life.

❧

SUPERNATURAL VS. INSTANTANEOUS

*Don't confine God to the instantaneous
and miss the supernatural.*

After people have received prayer for healing in a healing line and see no immediate results, they many times cast away their faith and think they didn't receive their healing.

Actually, they don't fully understand healing. Everything that is supernatural isn't always instantaneous.

Mary, the mother of Jesus, had a supernatural experience of the Holy Spirit placing within her womb the Word of God in seed form. Jesus was the Word of God made flesh. For nine months, Mary carried that baby in her womb. He was completely supernatural, yet she didn't deliver Him instantaneously. The seed had to grow.

Give the Word in you time to grow and produce a harvest. The seed of God's healing Word in you is supernatural and will bring results, but not always instantaneously.

Jesus ministered supernatural healing power to the sick, yet they weren't always instantly healed. The blind man had to wash the clay off first in the pool of water. The ten lepers had to make their way to the priest before they saw any physical change. Another blind man saw men as trees before he saw them as men, yet all of them experienced the supernatural.

We have mistakenly linked the words "supernatural" and "instantaneously" together and thought that one was incomplete without the other, but that just isn't so. Just because your healing doesn't manifest instantaneously doesn't mean that the supernatural isn't at work in you!

Don't limit God and you, too, will experience the supernatural.

ENFORCING
THE VICTORY

It's the one who falls who has the opportunity to rise.

A woman preacher related the story of watching a boxing match on television and realized that one of the contenders in the fight was born again. He gave a little bit of his testimony before the fight, so the preacher undoubtedly decided he would be the one to root for.

As the fight started, this preacher began praying in tongues for the boxer and saying, "Lord help your child to win this match. You can't let Your man lose!"

As the fight proceeded to the third round, a message flashed on the screen and announced that the fight was prerecorded, and it named the Christian boxer as the winner. The preacher admitted how foolish she felt praying for a fight that had already been fought.

I then thought how foolish Christians must look to God when uttering prayers asking God to help them win a fight that Jesus has already won for them! Our job is not to fight again the fight that Jesus has already won. Our job is to enforce with our faith the victory that He obtained for us.

You don't need to pray for that which already belongs to you. Healing already belongs to you — just receive it! I Peter 2:24 records, *"...by whose stripes ye WERE healed."* Just receive it!

Your healing doesn't depend on God's ability to heal, but on your ability to receive. He has all ability, but your ability to receive either causes healing to flow or hinders it from flowing.

After the message had flashed on the screen telling the outcome of the fight, the preacher said how much more she enjoyed the fight, knowing the outcome. When she saw that Christian man get knocked to the mat, she didn't worry in the least, because she knew since he was the winner, he would undoubtedly get up.

We should go through life with the same joy, assurance, and carefree attitude because we know our outcome. God is so awesome in power that He knows the beginning from the end. He already knows the outcome of mankind and the human race. Then, through what He tells us in His Word, He flashes that information of the outcome upon the screen of our lives so we can encounter this life of faith with absolute joy, peace, and assurance, knowing full well that He is our victory — victory is ours!

Colossians 2:15 tells us, *"And having spoiled principalities and powers, he made a shew of them openly, TRIUMPHING over them in it."*

Your opponent, the devil, will try to knock you down on the mat of defeat, but take heart and courage; you must rise — the victor always does!

> *The steps of a good man are ordered by the Lord: and he delighteth in his way. Though he fall, he shall not be utterly cast down: for the Lord upholdeth him with his hand.*
>
> Psalm 37:23, 24

Every believer who falls to the mat must rise, for the victory Jesus has already won for him demands it.

D a y   4 2

❧

DIVINE BOLDNESS

*"...grant unto thy servants, that with all boldness
they may speak thy word."*

Acts 4:29

Many believers assume they need more faith when
what they actually need is more boldness!

We are taught in the Bible that faith comes by
hearing the Word of God, so we know how to get faith.
Yet the apostles knew that boldness would carry their
faith into an arena they had not been before: the
arena of signs and wonders.

It takes divine boldness to look the opposition in
the eye, declare the Word to the opposer, and stand
still while the Word does its work.

How did the apostles get more boldness? They
asked God for it.

It is the same kind of boldness that caused David to
run toward Goliath. It is the same kind of boldness
that allowed Daniel to sleep in peace among the lions.
It is the same kind of boldness Jesus had that allowed
Him to sleep in a sinking boat.

Heaven's boldness doesn't react to tests; it controls
them — with the response of faith!

Ask for it today — it's yours for the asking.

❦

A LOVE PROBLEM

"...faith which worketh by love."

Galatians 5:6

Too often believers think they have a faith problem, so they seek to gain more faith when, in reality, they have a love problem!

Faith works by love, and if your faith is not gaining what you desire, check to see if there's a problem with your love walk. If your love walk is faulty, your faith walk will be faulty.

Are there any grudges, resentment, unforgiveness, or ill feelings toward someone in your life? All these are "leaks" in the "pipeline of faith."

The big problem missed by most people is their love walk toward God. Has God requested you to do something for Him, and have you been disobedient to do it? Any area of disobedience to God or His Word means you are not walking in complete love toward Him.

Any step outside of love is sin. Any step taken away from love is a step made toward sin. Ask the Holy Spirit to reveal any area where there has been a lack of love on your part. He is faithful to help us with this.

Even those who have done a great injustice to you in life must be fully forgiven without your harboring any ill feeling or thoughts against them.

If you are seemingly unable to forgive someone,

ask Jesus to help you forgive the person, and make the choice to forgive. Pray for God's blessings to be upon that person and then watch ill feelings and unforgiveness bow to love.

Healing is not promised to anyone who is walking outside a life of love. Make love your great quest!

EVIL SPEAKING

You will reap in your own body what you sow
into the Body of Christ.

A minister recounted a testimony of a woman in his congregation who was in the final stages of a terminal illness. He and the church elders gathered around her in her hospital bed to pray for her healing and anoint her with oil according to James 5:14, 15.

The minister exhorted the sister that although she might not have any sin in her life, if she did, that would be an excellent time to confess it before God's healing power would be able to flow in her body.

After a few moments, she motioned to the pastor and told him the Spirit of God had revealed to her that her evil speaking had opened the door for this disease to come upon her. She confessed, "Through my evil speaking I have sowed cancer in the Body of Christ and have therefore reaped cancer in my own body."

She asked the pastor and elders to forgive her, and they did. They laid hands on her and prayed, and God's power went through her, instantly healing her and raising her up!

The following Sunday, she repented to the congregation, received their forgiveness, and a move of God began in the church.

It is a serious matter to speak ill against God, His ministers, and Jesus' sheep, for whom He died. But if we would judge ourselves, we would not be judged, according to I Corinthians 11:31.

LIVE RICH

Let us live as rich as we are!

How it must grieve the heart of God to see how His children live so far beneath what He has provided for them. Poverty, depression, and sickness all wage war successfully against His children.

It should not be this way, because the Father *"...hath blessed us with ALL spiritual blessings in heavenly places in Christ"* (Ephesians 1:3). We have access to everything heaven possesses!

Why, then, do so many believers live lives of constant struggle?

Because they remain ignorant of what heaven has provided for them.

Spiritual enlightenment is the greatest need of the Church: seeing what is yours because of what Christ did for you and walking in it.

Enlightenment comes through the Word of God, with the Spirit of God teaching you.

In the story of the prodigal son, the elder son was jealous of the blessings the father was bestowing upon the wayward younger son who had returned home. He put a ring on his hand, shoes on his feet, killed the fatted calf, and held a feast.

The elder brother was so angry when he saw the blessings being heaped on his brother, he wouldn't even go to the feasting place. His father begged him to participate, but he responded by reminding him about all the long years he had served him faithfully, yet he had never received the kind of treatment his wayward brother was receiving.

The loving response of the father was, *"...all that I have is thine"* (Luke 15:31).

He had free access to his father's ring, but he never put it on. He could have had any clothing his father possessed; he just never wore it.

It never pays to become jealous of the blessings another believer is receiving, because you have the same Father if you are born again — and all that He has is yours, too.

Jealousy will only keep you outside of where the feast is taking place.

Live as rich as you are and feast at the table spread by the Father, who still calls, saying, *"All that I have is thine."*

THE EVIL PUPPETEER

Satan doesn't want attention through recognition;
he wants attention through control.

When working a puppet, the puppeteer never wants to be seen, for that would only take way from the performance. He desires only to control the actions of the puppet.

In the same respect, Satan wants to dominate your life without your knowing it is he. He loves it when you mistake his actions for people's actions.

In fact, if you recognize him as the culprit behind all your hardships, it will be difficult for him to keep you in them. He wants only to control your life while going completely unnoticed.

Too often believers don't recognize the actions of Satan when a sickness or a disease attacks their body. They just go to the doctor, get the medical name for it, and say that's the problem.

If you were to suggest to them that this is the work of darkness, a stroke of Satan himself, they would even defend their sickness. "Oh no," they would say, "the doctor told me it is such-and-such sickness."

Did you ever notice that every medical problem has a name? But that doesn't mean that every problem is medical, and that doesn't mean that hell didn't birth it.

Too many believers focus on the medical cause

while Satan laughs, because that medical name throws a cloak over him, disguising him as its source. Don't let the medical name hide from your view that sickness is still a work of darkness.

Satan is a spiritual being, and all the works of darkness are birthed from the spiritual realm. To successfully defeat him, he must be dealt with on a spiritual level. It takes the Word of God to successfully drive back and defeat every dark work.

I have heard born-again believers deny that Satan had anything to do with the sickness that had been in their bodies for years. They've said, "Oh, my body is just malfunctioning."

The Syrophenician woman who had no covenant with God and knew nothing about spiritual things said, "My daughter has a devil!"

Even a heathen woman knew the devil's work when she saw it. The Church needs to wise up and recognize it, too!

As long as you fail to recognize that Satan is the source of that sickness, you will bow to that sickness instead of driving it back and defeating it with the Word of God!

❦

GOD'S WILLINGNESS

"Who forgiveth all thine iniquities;
who healeth all thy diseases."

Psalm 103:3

We have great faith in God's willingness to forgive, but some don't always have great faith in God's willingness to heal. In fact, God's willingness can never be an issue again in either matter, because He has already paid the price for man's salvation and healing! It is paid in full, and it can never be undone.

Even if God did become unwilling to save someone, it's too late! The price for salvation has been paid.

Even if God did become unwilling to heal someone, it's too late! Healing was paid for at Calvary, so God's willingness never enters into it.

He was so willing to save and heal everyone, He sent His own Son to do the job to make sure it was done right!

God's willingness is as unchangeable as He is. God wills for everyone to be saved and for everyone to be healed.

Someone may argue, "If it is God's will to heal everyone, why isn't everyone healed?" The two reasons why people aren't healed is: They don't know it is available, or they don't receive it.

Notice Psalm 103:3, *"Who forgiveth ALL thine iniqui-*

ties; who healeth ALL thy diseases."

God's forgiving power reaches to all iniquities, and God's healing power reaches to all diseases.

His healing power is as far-reaching as His forgiving power. You receive His healing power in the same way you receive His forgiving power. Believe for His healing power just as easily as you believe for His forgiving power, and His healing power will flow to you just as freely as His forgiving power flows to you.

❦

KEEPING YOUR EYES ON JESUS

The wind and the waves only became a hindrance to Peter's walk on the water when he gave them his attention.

So many things in life shout for our attention. Life's obligations speak loudly in our ears. The demands of children are great. Our jobs require much time. Yet, in the midst of all this, we must learn to keep God and His Word at the center of our affections and as the focus of our gaze.

Cultivate the ability to shut out all that would draw your attention away from Christ. If we learn to do this in the everyday details of life, it will aid us in doing it when we are encompassed in tests or trials.

The biggest temptation in the midst of any test or trial is to take your eyes off Jesus. The enemy wants you to look elsewhere, because when you see Jesus, it is impossible to see defeat. But any other place you gaze will only cause you to sink below that which you once walked upon.

It wasn't water that was holding up Peter; it was faith. Water holds up no one, but faith upholds all things.

When you operate in faith, the water and all other opposition of Satan stay under your feet.

Don't be afraid of water, because with Jesus beside you, the waves become your home!

❦

GET OUT OF YOUR HEAD AND INTO YOUR HEART

If Satan gets you to operate from the mental arena,
he will defeat you.
The way to walk in victory is to operate
from the spiritual arena; then you
will seal his defeat in your life!

You keep yourself in the spiritual arena
through worship and praise.

Just as God is a three-part being (God the Father, God the Son, and God the Holy Spirit), we, being made in His image, are also three-part beings. We are a spirit (the heart of man); we have a soul (comprised of man's will, emotions, and mind); and we live in a body. These are the three arenas in the life of a man that he has to deal with.

The Bible teaches us that the body of man and the spirit of man are at enmity with each other. The body of man always wants to do things that violate the born-again spirit of man.

That's why Paul said, *"I keep under my body."* He knew if the body is given its liberty to rule a person's life, its unrestrained desires would take him away from the guidance of God's Spirit and lead him into hell. So the body and the spirit of man never agree.

The soul of man — his mind, will, and emotions — is the arena where either the body or the spirit wins the battle. The arena that the mind (soul) sides with is the arena that will dominate the man.

If the mind of man takes sides with his spirit, his spirit will dominate him; but if the mind of man takes sides with his body, his body will dominate him.

If the mind of man is unrenewed and educated only according to the knowledge of this world, the body will sway the mind of that man to follow it's yearnings, desires, and lusts.

But if a man's mind is renewed by the Word of God, at times of tests and trials, the renewed mind will take the counsel of the Word of God, allowing his spirit to guide him.

The devil wants you to live with your mind being your guide, for then he can dictate to it through the whims of this world. Satan can out-think the natural mind, so he knows if he can keep you operating out of the mental arena, he has already won.

But if you will make your mind take a back seat to the guidance of your recreated human spirit, Satan's defeat is sealed! He cannot operate through your spirit.

God operates through your spirit and Jesus has defeated Satan in the spiritual arena. By staying in that arena, victory will flow from your spirit, through your mind, and into your body.

When Satan's buffeting blows come continuously against your mind, how can you keep your mind from being swayed away from operating out of your spirit? Through worship and praise!

Make your lips do their work: *"His praise shall continually be in my mouth."* Praise and worship holds you in the arena of your spirit.

Worship from the heart will calm the effects of Satan's blows against your mind, rendering them ineffective.

Day 50

❧

HIGHER KNOWLEDGE

When a tree is cut down, its life source has been cut off, yet its limbs and branches remain green, appearing to be alive. Nevertheless, they are only symptoms of what used to be.

When the eye looks at a tree that has been cut down and is still green, it sees life. But when the mind looks at that same tree, it sees death, because the mind's knowledge goes beyond what the eye sees. The knowledge of the mind tells us that when we see a tree that has been cut down, it is dead, even though it may still be green.

In the same way, faith is a higher knowledge that operates beyond the knowledge of the eye.

When you tell sickness, disease, or pain to be removed (Mark 11:23), you have cut the tree from its life source. Although the "limbs" of symptoms may remain green, don't be concerned about them.

By keeping the death blow of the ax — your confession that the sickness or disease is cut off from your body — laid at the root of the tree, the limbs of pain and symptoms will weaken daily, losing strength and vitality. They will soon droop and fall off to be trodden under the foot of man.

❧

DEAD TO SIN

In the same way you resist the temptation to sin,
you resist the temptation to be sick.

Sickness is to the body what sin is to the spirit.

Satan comes to every believer and tries to get him to receive thoughts to sin and do wrong. Sometimes the temptation is slight and is easily resisted, but at other times the force of the temptation is greater and persists for a longer period of time.

Whether the temptation is long or short, continue to resist it! Tell Satan, "I will not think on that thought. I will not commit that act of sin with my mind against my God. I will not!"

It's the same with pains or symptoms. They are only temptations to be sick. Whether they are short-lived or persist in their attack, your stand against them must remain the same. Just as you resist the thought to sin, resist the symptoms to be sick!

How are we able to resist symptoms and pain successfully every time?

Who his own self bare our sins in his own body
on the tree, that WE, BEING DEAD TO SINS,
should live unto righteousness: by whose stripes
ye were healed.

I Peter 2:24

This verse tells me I am dead to sin. Sin can't affect a dead person!

Since I am dead to sin, I am also dead to what sin birthed: sickness!

Healing evangelist John Alexander Dowie, founder of Zion, Illinois, stated that sickness is the foul offspring of its mother, Sin, and its father, Satan.

Since I am dead to sin, I am also dead to sin's foul offspring, sickness!

When pains come, tell them, "No, I am dead to you. You can't touch me." Whether they persist for a short or a long time, resist them as you would resist sin, and you will be their slave no longer!

❦

THE SLEEP OF FAITH

It is vain for you to rise up early, to take rest late,
to eat the bread of
[anxious] toil; for HE GIVES [BLESSINGS]
TO HIS BELOVED IN SLEEP.

Psalm 127:2 (The Amplified Bible)

The believer who goes to sleep in faith can be assured of help from God even in his sleep!

To stay awake and worry about that financial problem or that wayward loved one only serves to keep God from being able to do what He wants to do for you. Your losing sleep over the tests and trials of life won't fix them. Cast them over on God, and refuse to let them be your care. God is unable to help you until you cast every care upon Him, and if you have really cast that care upon Him, believing that He is well able to fix it, you will quit worrying about it.

In the same respect, worrisome, fearful, restless nights worrying about your body will only serve to hold that sickness and disease in place. One of the most valuable things we must learn is that we have to sleep in faith, even if the storm is still raging.

Jesus was masterful at that. When He was in the boat asleep while the storm was raging, He wasn't concerned about it. If the boat sank, no worry. He knew He could just walk on the water and get to where He was going.

Tell God and the devil that you're going to sleep in faith. God always meets faith, even if it is in your sleep. If you're sleeping in faith, the above verse tells us that He gives His blessings to us as we sleep.

Healing is a blessing, isn't it? If you'll go to sleep in faith, the healing power of God will work in your body as you do. Tell God you believe that because it is His Word.

What if you go to sleep but are awakened by fearful thoughts or dreams that disturb you? Pull your Bible out and read this verse to yourself and to the devil, and tell him that you refuse to take any other sleep than peaceful, blessing-filled sleep.

You might ask, "What if interrupted, restless sleep persists?" You be persistent, too — persistent with the Word. The Word always wins, just keep at it! Make the Word of God your pillow.

Victory is sure, and the sleep victory gives is sweet!

Day 53

❧

HINDERED PRAYERS

Love is what makes prayers audible in the ears of God.

I Peter 3:7 tells us that husbands can hinder their prayers from being answered when they don't honor their wives.

If husbands' prayers can be hindered, don't you think that wives' prayers can also be hindered if they don't give the proper honor to their husbands?

God doesn't require something of one person and not require it of another in a matter such as this.

In Ephesians 5:33, The Amplified Bible reads:

> *...let the wife see that she respects and reverences her husband [that she notices him, regards him, honors him, prefers him, venerates and esteems him; and that she defers to him, praises him, and loves and admires him exceedingly].*

We would even be correct in instructing the husband to show the same respect for the wife. Wouldn't the home that practices this respect every day be heaven on Earth?

"But what if my spouse doesn't treat me like that?"

That doesn't release you from your responsibility to the Word to treat him or her like that. You obey this scripture because it's an instruction to you from God, not because someone else does it first.

There is a lot of sickness in believers' bodies because they don't treat their spouses as they should!

Too many Christians have other family members running their marriages instead of submitting to their spouses.

If you want the healing power and blessings of God in your life, you must line up with the Word of God in every area of your life. You must examine your attitude, thoughts, and behavior regarding your marriage.

Do you allow yourself to think unlovely thoughts about your spouse? Shame on you! Judge yourself so you won't be judged!

Do you surround yourself with friends or family who are critical of your spouse? You had better correct that so your prayers will be unhindered.

The fellowship of the Father and His blessings are too precious to allow anything to hinder their flow.

A marriage of love is the result of seeds of love having been sown into it.

Day 54

❧

LOVING THE WORD

*"Unless thy law had been my delights,
I should then have perished in mine affliction."*

Psalm 119:92

"Who so despiseth the word shall be destroyed..."

Proverbs 13:13

If despising the Word will destroy, loving the Word will deliver.

Many Christians would shudder at the suggestion that they despised the Word. "I've never been guilty of despising the Word," they would protest.

Think back: Has God ever told you to do something, and you disobeyed? That's called "despising the word."

If you had loved that word from the Lord, you would have obeyed promptly.

We are prompt to obey the words God speaks to us if we like them and they fit into our plans. If, however, He should dare to give us words that are not to our liking, slothfulness, apathy, and sometimes blatant disobedience soon become our companions.

If we seek to receive the blessings of the Father, we would do well to see to it that we are delighting in His every word!

Day 55

❦

TWO REALMS

The realm you yield to is the realm that will rule you.

There is the realm of God, and there is the realm of Satan. In God's realm is everything good, blessed, and life-giving. In Satan's realm is everything bad, harmful, and evil.

The influence of Satan's realm in this world is easily seen. Hate, murder, abuse, theft, drunkenness, and unspeakable sins are all the order of the day.

Why was Satan ever permitted to have his influence upon this Earth?

Adam permitted it. God gave Adam the authority to oversee the Garden of Eden when he was placed there. God gave him dominion.

When Adam succumbed to Satan, he not only lost his fellowship with God; through that act he also turned the dominion of this Earth over to Satan — the dominion that was once his!

Therefore, Satan is now the "god of this world," according to II Corinthians 4:4. Adam's sin is what opened the door for Satan's realm to manifest in this world.

But we are not without hope, because Jesus said that although Satan came into the world to kill, steal, and destroy, He Himself came that we might have life, and have it more abundantly (John 10:10).

Every person who is born again has that abundant

107

life within himself or herself. The more they yield to that life, the more abundantly it will manifest through them into a hurting world.

Although Satan has dominion of this world because of Adam's sin, he no longer has dominion over the believer, because Jesus stripped him of his power on Calvary. We are cleansed by Jesus' blood, and that blood has overcome the enemy.

We have overcome Satan *"...by the blood of the Lamb, and by the word of* (our) *testimony..."* (Revelation 12:11).

Our testimony about the blood is, "Through the blood, I have overcome Satan, and I am no longer subject to his realm that is being manifested upon this Earth."

"I have been translated from the power of darkness that is at work in this world and into the kingdom of God's dear Son" (Colossians 1:13).

Now that believers no longer belong to Satan's kingdom and are free from the effects of Satan's realm, how does Satan manage to defeat so many Christians in so many different areas of their lives?

He gets them to yield to him.

He makes lack appear to be the norm for this world. But it isn't the norm for heaven or heaven's children, so rebuke it! You have been delivered from that old kingdom!

You receive the flu, "Because it's been going around, you know." It isn't going around in God's kingdom, so rebuke it!

If heaven doesn't give it to you, you've got no business with it. Only take what comes from your heavenly Father.

How do you get the possessions and the blessings of heaven to flow through your life?

Yield to them. Your words, thoughts, and actions are all ways through which you yield.

If your words, thoughts, and actions reflect doubt,

worry, and unbelief, you have just yielded to Satan's realm, and that is what will manifest. But if your words, thoughts, and actions are guided by the Word of God, you are yielding to God's realm, and His realm will manifest in your life.

Day 56

🍂

Casting
Your Cares

Cast ALL your cares upon Him!

Many Christians have failed to receive their healing because they worry. Worries keep your eyes focused upon the problem, holding the answer away from your reach.

> *Casting the WHOLE of your care [all your anxieties, all your worries, all your concerns, once and for all] on Him; for He cares for you affectionately, and cares about you watchfully.*

> I Peter 5:7 (The Amplified Bible)

Could you really believe this verse and continue to worry? Absolutely not!

Worry is disobedience to God's Word, and disobedience is sin.

When thoughts and fears bombard, how do you keep from taking them?

You must say, "No, Satan, that isn't my thought. I have no care, because I have cast it upon God."

Many will have to break their "habit" of worrying. Some have taken it up as a pastime, a hobby in life, not realizing how offensive and sinful it is to God; but the Word will help you walk free from it as you obey I Peter 5:7.

If I were searching through my kitchen for something to cook for supper, but my husband called from the office and said, "Don't cook supper tonight. I'll pick up something for us to eat at the drive-through," wouldn't I look crazy if I continued to hunt through the kitchen, wringing my hands, wondering what to make for supper?

By acting that way, I would be saying that my husband is a liar and wouldn't do what he said he would do. I would be totally disregarding his word.

In the same respect, there are people who must totally disregard what God has already said to them in the Bible. He tells us not to worry or take any care in life, because He is caring for us. Yet they wring their hands with worry and wonder what to do. How faithless that must appear in God's sight!

The Christian life is sweet and full of rewards. Make the decision to enjoy your life! Fill it with God and His Word, and watch how well God will take care of you when you free yourself from the cares and worries of life.

> *Commit your way to the Lord — roll and repose [each care of] your load on Him; trust (lean on, rely on and be confident) also in Him, and HE WILL BRING IT TO PASS.*
>
> Psalm 37:5 (The Amplified Bible)

Continue to leave the care with Him, for only then is He able to bring His promise to pass in your life.

❦

A NEW REALM

Calvary was the realm of Satan losing authority over our realm!

Satan is a defeated foe. Jesus' death and resurrection sealed his doom forever and brought you into a whole new realm of living.

The only stipulation to maintaining victory is not looking back at the realm from which you have been delivered. "...*Old things are passed away; behold, ALL things are become new*" (II Corinthians 5:17). Hebrews 11:15 tells us that if Abraham would have been mindful of the land he had come out of, he would have had opportunity to return to it.

Is any of the "old" life still clinging to you? Focus your spiritual eyes on the "new" — the life Jesus has provided for you — and refuse to be bound by the "old."

We lose what is in God's realm by fixing our eyes on what is in Satan's realm.

The realm you see and talk about is the realm that will manifest in your life. If you want more of heaven's manifestations, think and talk about that realm continually.

Everything God has in His realm, that's what I say I have in mine!

Sickness is non-existent in God's realm; therefore, it has no right to exist in my realm!

Day 58

❧

POSSESSING
YOUR HEALING

"...First the blade, then the ear, after that the full corn in the ear."
Mark 4:28

Often, healing occurs through a process. The person recovers daily as he or she walks in faith.

Abraham was called to leave his homeland to possess a land that God had already given him. It was God's job to provide a possession, but Abraham's job to possess it. He wasn't translated to that place; he had to walk there, one step at a time.

Your healing is a possession provided by God, but you must possess it, one step at a time.

Faith can translate a person from one place to the next, but all people are not translated into their healing in a moment of time. Some travel into it, one faith step at a time. As each step is taken, they draw nearer to the possession that is already theirs.

The Word of God teaches us the process through which healing often comes: *"...First the blade, then the ear and then the full corn in the ear."*

You may only see a "blade" of improvement, but don't become discouraged or bitter, because if you continue to believe and hold fast to your confession of faith, the "blade" is a sign that the full corn in the ear is on its way!

One of the best things for the believer to learn is the daily, consistent "walk of faith." We run from time to time, but even that is done one step at a time.

Day 59

❦

PROSPERITY
OF THE SOUL

*"Beloved, I wish above all things that thou mayest
prosper and be in health, even as thy soul prospereth."*
III John 2

The degree of prosperity and health one walks in is
in direct proportion to the prosperity of his or her
soul.

The person who stays full of the Word of God
through daily fellowship and meditation and allows the
Word of God to govern his thoughts and actions makes
himself available to greater prosperity and ongoing
health.

Many Christians seek to gain their health through
the prayers of someone else or through a prayer line.
Although these are valid means of receiving ministry,
the Word's ongoing instructions are for believers to
become prosperous in their souls.

In fact, the believer who takes the time to build up
his spirit and mind is one who will not lose what he
gains through a prayer line. Those who are negligent
in the development of their souls, on the other hand,
are less likely to maintain what they may have received
through a prayer line.

*"Thy word is a lamp unto my feet, and a light unto my
path"* (Psalm 119:105).

Through God's Word, illumination is given to
those who once walked in the darkness of lack and

sickness.

Through His Word, "the light of the word" shines abundance and health into your life!

The Word of God is your answer to every problem in life.

"He sent his word, and healed them..." (Psalm 107:20).

Day 60

ॐ

CAPTURING
EVERY THOUGHT

*Victory will reign only in the life of the one whose mind
is his servant instead of his master!*

*"Casting down imaginations, and every high thing
that exalteth itself against the knowledge of God..."*
II Corinthians 10:5

The greatest battle a believer ever faces is the battle to keep his thinking in line with the Word of God. Imaginations of defeat and what "might be" tomorrow will keep all your "todays" bound.

All believers must learn to cast down every imagination that is against the Word of God, because the imagination directly affects the will of man.

The will to continue or quit is guided by one's imagination. If a person sees himself victorious, he continues; but if he sees himself going under, he quits.

The things you allow yourself to think about today will guide all of your tomorrows.

Too many people "play" with thoughts they don't realize will become their destruction. No holy life can ever be lived through the person whose mind is uncontrolled.

Restraints upon the thought life are imperative to live in victory.

A sick person cannot allow himself the luxury of imagining "the worst."

Satan will try to energize the mind with unholy imaginations, but they must be cast down!

The best way to drop something is to pick up something else in its place. When Satan gives you thoughts of your pending doom, cast them down by taking up the Word of God and speaking it to him and yourself.

II Corinthians 10:5 tells us to bring *"...into captivity EVERY thought to the obedience of Christ."* To successfully obey these instructions, every time a thought comes into your mind, take it captive and examine it.

If it is in line with the Word of God, release it to run free in your life. If it is against the Word, never give it a place in you.

Every thought you take is either a battle lost or a victory gained!

Victory will reign only in the life of the one whose mind is his servant instead of his master!

SUGGESTED READINGS ON DIVINE HEALING

Christ the Healer
F. F. Bosworth

Healing Promises (scriptures)
Kenneth and Gloria Copeland

There's a Healer in the House
Dr. Ed Dufresne

Faith That Makes a Demand on the Anointing
Dr. Ed Dufresne

Bodily Healing and the Atonement
T. J. McCrossan

Healing Belongs to Us
Kenneth E. Hagin

Seven Things You Should Know About Divine Healing
Kenneth E. Hagin

The Key to Scriptural Healing
Kenneth E. Hagin

Jesus the Healer
E. W. Kenyon

The Life of Faith
Mrs. C. Nuzum

The Gospel of Healing
A. B. Simpson

Balm of Gilead
Lilian B. Yeomans

Healing From Heaven
Lilian B. Yeomans

Health and Healing
Lilian B. Yeomans

The Great Physician
Lilian B. Yeomans

All the above books may be ordered through their publishers
or from Ed Dufresne Ministries.

A Sinner's Prayer
To Receive Jesus As Savior

Dear Heavenly Father:

I come to You in the Name of Jesus.
Your Word says, *"...him that cometh to me
I will in no wise cast out"* (John 6:37).

So I know You won't cast me out;
But You will take me in,
And I thank You for it.

You said in your Word, *"...if thou shalt confess
with thy mouth the Lord Jesus, and shall believe
in thine heart that God hath raised him from the dead,
THOU SHALT BE SAVED...For whosoever shall call upon
the name of the Lord shall be saved"* (Romans 10:9, 13).

I believe in my heart that
Jesus Christ is the Son of God.
I believe Jesus died for my sins
and was raised from the dead
so I could be in rightstanding with God.
I am calling upon His Name, the Name of Jesus,
so I know, Father, that You save me now.

Your Word says, *"...with the heart
man believeth unto righteousness;
and with the mouth confession is made
unto salvation"* (Romans 10:10).
I do believe with my heart,
And I confess Jesus now as my Lord.
Therefore, I am saved!
Thank You, Father.

Please write us and let us know that you
have just been born again.
When you write,
ask to receive our salvation booklets.

To contact us, please write to:
Ed Dufresne Ministries
P.O. Box 1010
Murrieta, CA 92564

Visit our website at: **www.eddufresne.org**